ART WITH A STORY 2

Original Art.
Original Fiction.

by

John Nieman

Gotham Books

30 N Gould St.
Ste. 20820, Sheridan, WY 82801
https://gothambooksinc.com/

Phone: 1 (307) 464-7800

Published by Gotham Books (October 20, 2023)

ISBN: 979-8-88775-501-4 (P)
ISBN: 979-8-88775-502-1 (E)

Because of the dynamic nature of the Internet, any web addresses or links contained in this book may have changed since publication and may no longer be valid.

The views expressed in this work are solely those of the author and do not necessarily reflect the views of the publisher, and the publisher hereby disclaims any responsibility for them.

Table of Contents

For Jack,

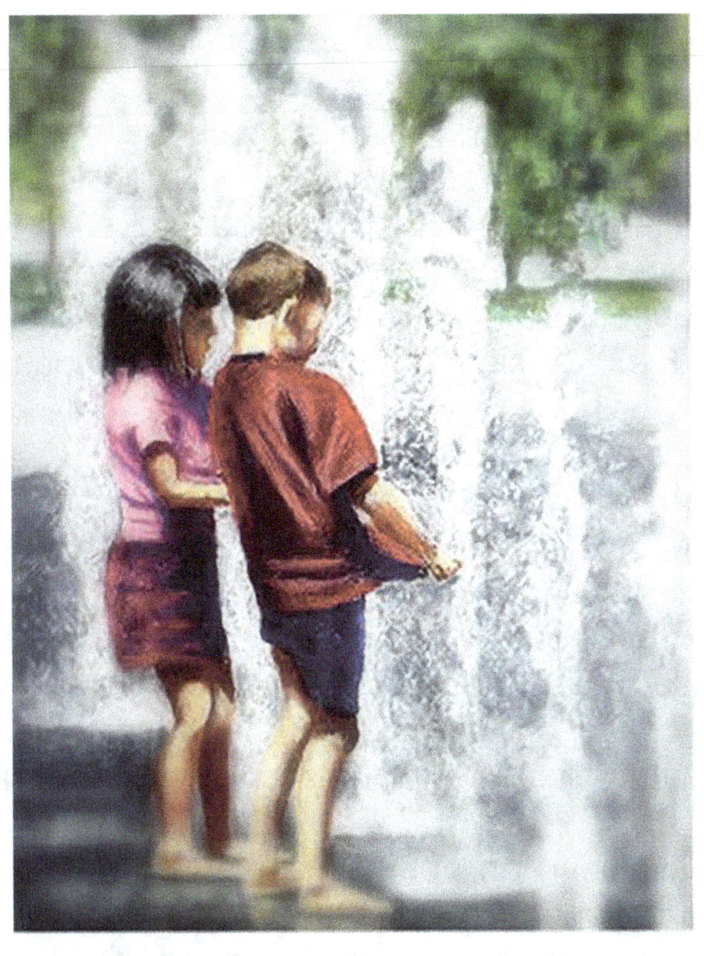

Let's Get Wet

Perhaps at a very early age, we learn the seductive allure and the spontaneous thrill of water.

It happens every time we dive into a less-than-warm swimming pool. It happens when we are caught in a rainstorm without an umbrella. It happens any day when a sprinkler unexpectedly showers us in a business suit.

For Kiki and Mack Devlin, it happened across from Notre-Dame Basilica in Montreal, Canada. Mr. and Mrs. Devlin had organized the family trip as a way to expand their kids' take on the world. Like the erudite Clark Griswold, Mr. Devlin had envisioned a chockablock trip of cathedrals, museums, and fine cuisine. Both kids had gamely followed along in the adult footsteps, but the nonstop sightseeing had clearly taken its toll on the kids.

"Do we have to?" eight-year-old Mack asked his dad as he plopped down on the concrete bench.

"It's too hot," his younger sister, Kiki, added.

Mr. Devlin looked at the church tower across the street and started ticking off the appeal of this site. "A, it was built in 1829. B, it's the basilica for the entire city. C, it has world-famous mosaics and stained glass."

"What's a mosaic?" little Kiki asked.

"Some churchy art thing," her brother correctly guessed. "How long?"

"Ten minutes tops," Mr. Devlin promised.

"Can we just rest here?" Kiki looked at her mother with her best sad-eyed, please-please-please, pleading expression.

Mrs. Devlin looked around the courtyard and saw no imminent dangers—a few tourists, a few fountains, and a short line to get into the basilica.

Young Mack, sensing an opening, knew the magic words. "Mom, we won't talk to anyone. We won't take any candy. We won't wander away," he said, looking at the gushing street fountains a few feet from the bench, which, in his mind, hardly constitutes *wandering*. "Besides, it's Canada," the kid said. "People aren't so crazy here."

"Ten minutes," Mom answered. "I am trusting you."

When the couple walked away toward the cathedral doors, Mack overheard "Are you sure?" from his dad.

"Honey, they're tired," she wearily answered. As the couple walked into the basilica, she added, "Fact is, I'm tired too. Why don't you go ahead and look at the mosaics. I'll keep an eye on the kids from this window." She then perched in the vestibule and watched the spontaneous drama unfold.

Clearly, young Mack was transfixed by the splash of the nearby fountains. There were at least six or seven waterspouts jetting from the concrete, and no older person seemed attracted to them. Some looked at maps. Some looked at guidebooks. Only Mack saw the fountains.

"Are you really hot?" he asked his younger sister. She nodded yes. He pointed to the gushing waters. And then, like any eight-year-old with a silly, mischievous master plan, he started to giggle.

"Let's get wet." He held out his hand gallantly to his younger sister. She looked back at the basilica, wiped a drop of sweat from her forehead, and followed.

Within minutes, they danced through the six fountains. At first, like a game, they tried to elude the droplets of water. After a few slalom runs, they gave up and freely accepted the cold shower with glee. It was so refreshing. It was so thrilling. It was so surprising to see their mom and dad now standing on the perimeter of the gushing springs, viewing their two kids laughing as they had never done on this trip.

"Mack! Kiki! What's going on here?" Dad barked in the Hollywood voice of a dutiful dad.

We don't really have a time clock on these stories, but I would estimate there was at least six seconds of silence. At about the seventh second, Mom giggled and suggested to her husband, "Let's join them." She did. And then she looked back at her husband. "C'mon!" To everyone's surprise, Mr. Organization must have sensed that the family was somehow slipping away and eventually danced in the fountains in his J.Crew khakis and polo shirt—out of character, over-the-top, and definitely off the agenda.

On the way home from Montreal, all the family could talk about was the amazing family shower in Old Montreal. Fifteen years later, that is still the family legend. Somewhat surprisingly, Mr. Devlin now loves to relate the story with pride.

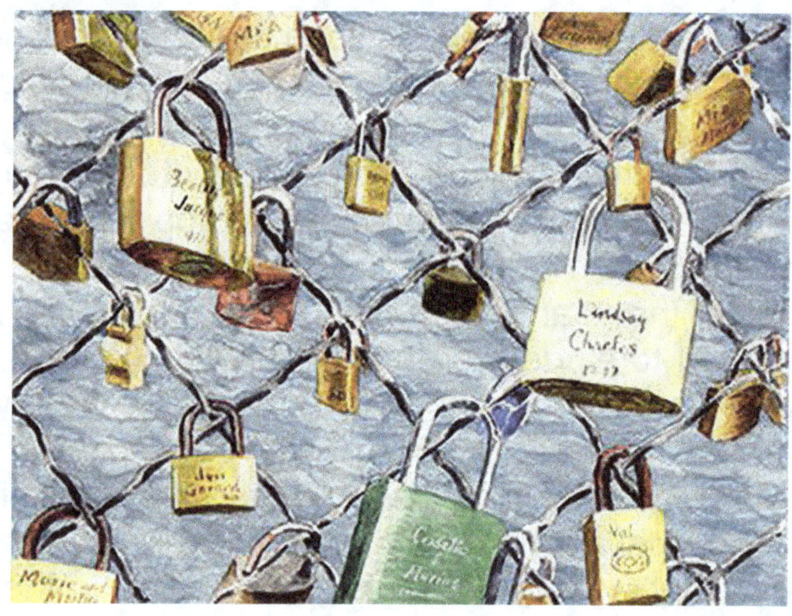

Throw Away the Key

It is not the most beautiful bridge in Paris.

However, Pont des Arts always offered a sense of romantic intrigue for Lindsay Buchanan. Ever since she had been relocated to the city of lights after gaining her MBA and landing a plum job at the Institut de France, where she managed the prizes and subsidies of over a hundred learned foundations, she had walked the bridge of padlocks every day. It was a nudging reminder that there was more to life than poring over daily dossiers of carefully worded grant proposals.

However, this had become her routine over the past several years. As you might expect, the trouble with the preceding sentence, at least in Lindsay's mind, was the word *routine.* As a twenty-eight-year-old attractive woman with an active brain, she could feel herself isolated into the regimen of success—especially when she walked across the bridge and saw gushing young couples giggle as they locked their romance into the fence and tossed the key with abandon into the Seine as a symbol of their unending love.

"Mademoiselle, s'il vous plait." She was occasionally requested by a camera-happy couple to click a happy snap of the padlocking event. Lindsay always complied, and the commemoration intensified her own internal doubts about whether such an outcome might ever occur in her life.

Today, she snapped a picture of a couple named Michelle and Pierre. They were from Marseille, in their midtwenties, fawningly, almost embarrassingly in love. Lindsay snapped a horizontal pose, a vertical pose, and a few extras of the two of them in a lip-lock.

After a "*Merci, merci,*" she nonchalantly walked to the fence and examined a few of the padlocks. Ironically, the largest, brightest one was a bronze lock inscribed with the names *Lindsay and Charles.* Charles? Charles who? Charlie? Chaz? Chuck? She could not identify a single suspect. Admittedly, she did think it was bit strange and desperate to connect the dots as such, but it was no weirder than having one's palm read and being told that there might be a Louis in her future.

That night, at a gala for the Académie Française, she met a professor called Charles Marchant, who taught literature at the Sorbonne. Unlike most chance encounters, he was not just another academic stiff who simply wanted to discuss comparative literature between Balzac and Camus. He had a wink and a twinkle in his eyes.

Unlike herself, Lindsay found herself laughing at his sarcastic comments about the pomposity of federal grant proposals. Atypically, she did not feel on point. She did not feel the need to be an apologist for elevated thought. She did not feel as if she were an ambassador for the Institut de France.

Well, you can guess what happened that night.

What is more remarkable is that it was not a one-night stand.

As I write this, they are now at the critical seven-month relationship pole.

Perhaps she sensed it. Perhaps he did. Either way, it was time to up the ante.

They crossed the Pont des Arts. With a magic marker, Lindsay pointed to her favorite place, wrote the inscription, and placed the padlock near her predecessors' relationship. If you look closely, you will see two Lindsay-and-Charles padlocks within a few feet of each other.

As she had experienced dozens of times, she asked an unsuspecting pedestrian to take a picture of the couple as they tossed the key into the deep, dark river called the Seine.

Love is wonderful.

Love is young.

Love is eternal.

Love it.

Believe it and toss away the key.

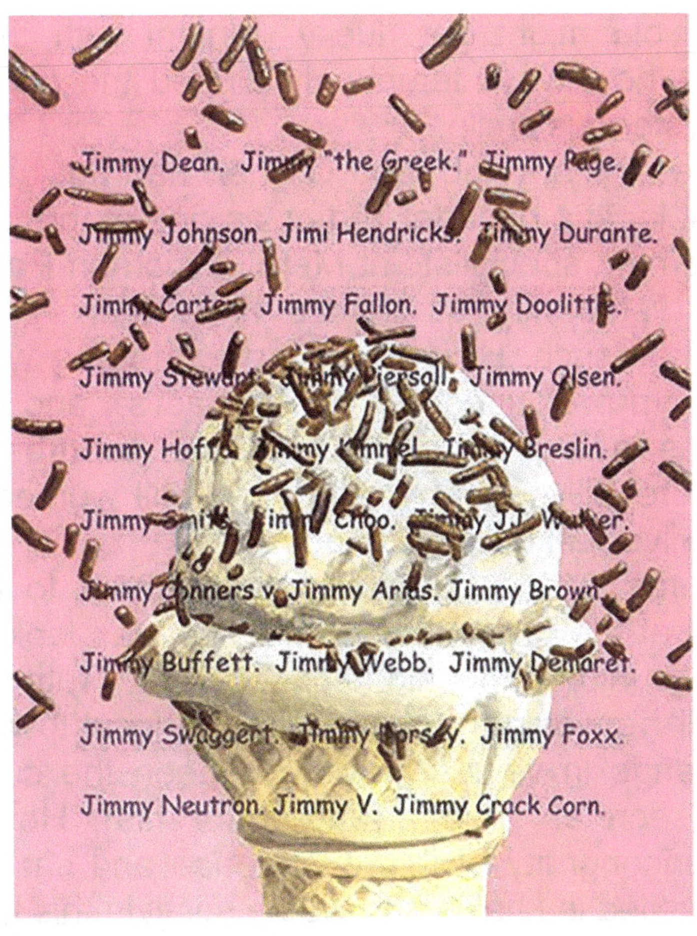

Jimmies
Watercolor
27 × 34
2013

Jimmies

He was baptized James Francis O'Brien, but everyone in the neighborhood always called him Jimmy.

It was the same shorthand with all his friends, who were known as Mickey, Billy, Tommy, and Joey. Maybe the nicknames stuck when they were first graders and played T-ball games together. Those carefree, lazy afternoons were normally followed by ice cream cones for the whole team, win or lose. (Their favorite variety from Burkie's Creamery was a vanilla double scoop dipped with those little chocolate thingies.)

"With jimmies?" the young teenage girl behind the counter would ask, and all the boys would giggle and point to Jimmy O'Brien as if the seven-year-old might get "lucky" tonight with the nubile high school senior, who always temptingly dipped the pure vanilla cone with a dark, mysterious smile.

That was fifteen years ago, and O'Brien had not been referred to as Jimmy for at least a decade. Today, as one of the most respected wealth management specialists at Merrill Lynch on Park Avenue, his business card listed him as James F. O'Brien; and his client's referred to him as such. His was now a high-flying world of Brooks Brothers suits, power lunches at Michael's, and weekends in Quogue. It was a far, far climb from the suburbs of Kenosha, Wisconsin, where Billy, Tommy, and Joey still worked within a six-mile radius of Silver Lake High School.

Those two eras and geographies were about to collide. When O'Brien landed at the Milwaukee airport, he was looking forward to this tenth-year reunion of his high school class. Truth be told, he did ponder whether he would truly fit in with the local townies. A telltale sign of the change in values may have been the curbside stretch limo that his secretary had arranged for him. However, he did recognize the incongruity of this experience and smiled at the fact that he had travelled in khakis and was a misfit in this luxo-vehicle.

An hour later, he checked into the Candlelight Suites and took a quick swim before meeting his name-tagged, vaguely still familiar male and female buddies.

"Millie!"

"Joey!"

"Susie!"

"Mickey!"

"Billy!"

"Tommy!

"Annie!"

"Jimmie!"

"Jimmie? Is that you, Jimmie?"

"Jimmie? Wow, you have grown up!"

Between dances and beers, O'Brien learned that Billy worked at the Midas Muffler shop, Susie was a schoolteacher in the next community, Mickey was in construction, and Billy was in jail. A few were simply missing in action. But most were at the reunion and were at least thirty pounds heavier and facially puffier.

This weight gain did not deter Joey, Mickey, and Tommy from inviting their friend to a calorie-laden ceremonial nightcap at Burkie's Creamery.

"What'll it be, boys?" The young teenage tart behind the counter knew how to tease her customers into ordering big. "How about something sweet? Something sinful? Something deep and dark and downright delicious?"

"You got jimmies?" Joey flirted back.

"Do I have jimmies?" The young woman behind the counter, who looked a little like Kim Kardashian, laughed out loud. "Do I have jimmies? I have jimmies in my dreams. I bring jimmies to completion . . . atop these creamy scoops." She knew what she was doing. All the boys ordered double vanillas or triple vanillas with an extra helping of jimmies. As she winked and prepared her treats, his once-upon-a-time friends elbowed O'Brien and giggled. "Jimmy. Jimmy. Jimmy." Unlike all the other Jameses, Jamesons, JPs, JBs, and JFs, Jimmy O'Brien did not feel above the moment. No, he rather enjoyed it. He was giggly, gabby, and goofy. And for at least this one brief weekend in ten long years, he enjoyed his roots before returning to the sorbet/gelato/granita/spumoni / sadly sophisticated world where he would once again and probably forever become known as James F. O'Brien.

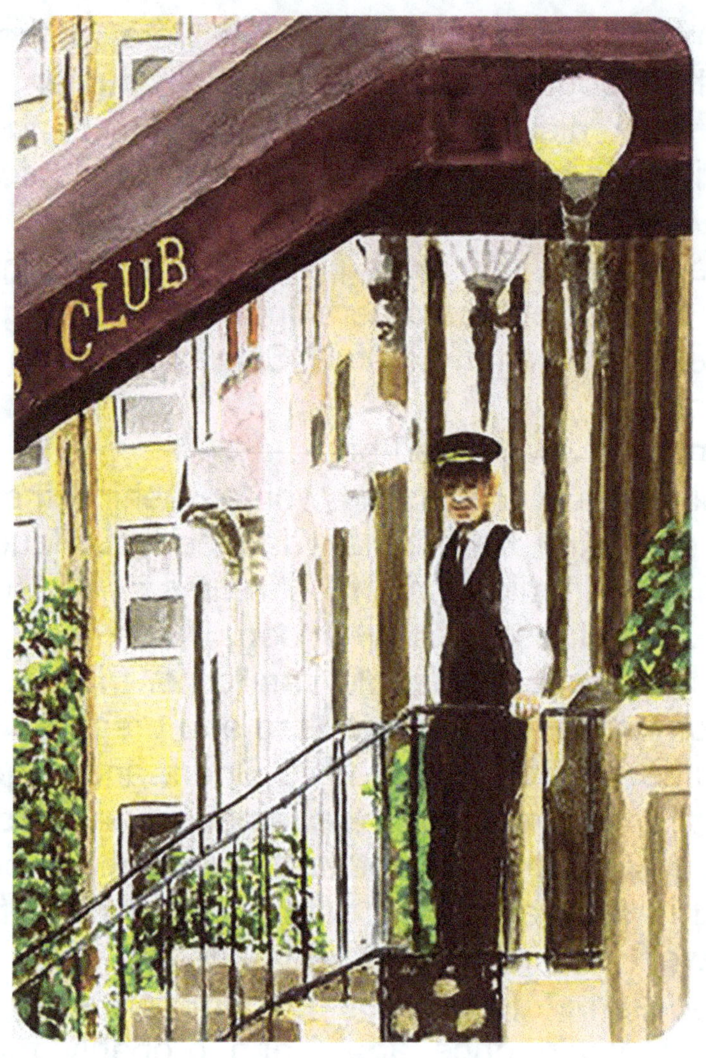

Welcome to the Club
Watercolor
16 × 22
2012

Welcome to the Club

There are bigger, more famous university clubs in Manhattan. However, few have as choice a location as the Williams Club on Madison and Thirty-Ninth, and none have a more elegant doorman than George Capek.

Every weekday morning, George would greet the breakfast visitors with a tip of the hat and his favorite expression, "Welcome to the club, Mr. McInerney, Mr. Case, Mr. Beschloss." He always thought it was important to recognize the members by name. Fortunately, he had a rather photographic memory. That talent was particularly appreciated on the weekends, when the members would bring outside guests and would be greeted by George as if they were the most important, significant players in Williams Club history.

By contrast, few members knew much about George Capek other than his hello. Few knew he had immigrated to the United States in the '70s from Prague. Fewer still knew he had escaped the communist Iron Curtain with his wife and young daughter in the middle of a November night, under a dangerous umbrella of Russian gunfire.

Like millions of Cold War refugees, the idea was to create a better life for one's family, and George and his wife had done that for their daughter, who graduated from Syracuse University five years ago and was now living in Chicago. His wife had become a sculptor of some note, while George continued to man the front door at the Williams Club for the past thirty years.

While he was proud of his accomplishments, his own lack of higher education always haunted him, especially since he had spent the bulk of his working lifetime around accomplished college grads, MBAs, and PhDs. Atypical of the illustrious alumni (Nathan Hale, Elia Kazan, Mika Brzezinski, George Steinbrenner), George Capek had only a high school diploma. Feeling this missing gap, the doorman asked to reduce his hours at the Williams Club six years ago. On those free Tuesdays and Thursdays, Mr. Capek took four college classes each day at Pace University (and at least a class or two over the summer).

This June 12, he had his 120-credit hours in psychology and graduated in a blue cap and gown from the university. His wife cried. His daughter flew in from Chicago and hooted from the auditorium when his name was called. George was somewhat embarrassed by all this hoopla, but in truth, it was his proudest day since immigrating to the USA. How great can a day be? How boundless the opportunities? How high is the sky?

George Capek was about to find out. His wife insisted on driving their Toyota and had reserved a special place for the man's graduation brunch. When she approached midtown Manhattan, he was somewhat curious about the destination. After all, he knew most of the surrounding restaurants. When they pulled up to the entrance of the Williams Club, the man was honestly dumbstruck to see thirty longtime members lined along the familiar stairs. At the bottom of the stairs, Mr. Carlin Conway greeted the employee/graduate and presented him with a certificate. On this day, June 12, it signified George Capek as an honorary member of the Williams Club.

"Your daughter told me about this last year," the club's president, Mr. Conway, told the longtime doorman. "And a bunch of fellow members wanted to come to greet you."

One by one, they repeated his favorite phrase, "Welcome to the Club, Mr. Capek." He slowly walked up the stairs and shook all their hands, then tipped his imaginary hat to all the familiar well-wishers. Then he took the hands of his wife and daughter and enjoyed his first brunch inside the mahogany walls of the exclusive club.

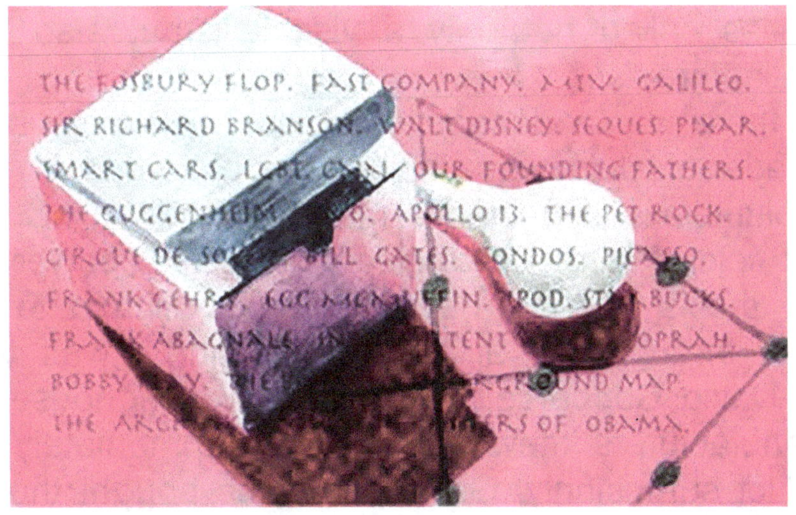

Thinking Outside the Box
Watercolor
30 × 20
2009

"Think Outside the Box"
(A quote from her recent speaking tour on the Mensa circuit)

Ever since high school, Melody Gerhardt had always been considered an iconoclastic, creative soul. An early telltale sign was the physically challenging dance performance she spearheaded at the Chestnut Hill Community Center, which was featured in the *Boston Herald*. "I just never thought a movement should be limited by two working legs," Gerhardt opined, citing the Special Olympics, wheelchair tennis, and paraplegic skydiving as inspirations. As you may know, this wheel-driven ballet, scored by Eumir Deodato, was eventually featured at Lincoln Center.

Her next foray into the unexpected was that controversial art show at Agora Gallery in Chelsea, New York. If you go back to the February 2002 issue of the *New Yorker*, you might find the rave review of the scrap metal collages she created from 9/11 materials called *Aftermath: 9/11*. Despite the vast publicity bump (and some negative backlash), what redeemed her was that any proceeds of the show would go to the fallen heroes of the NY disaster. At this point, she was called not only a visionary but also "American's youngest philanthropist."

And then there was a decade of silence. Put more accurately, it was a decade of discovery, higher education, and travel. She attended Columbia and gained a master's and a PhD in six short months. Her field of study: solar/electrical/nuclear power generation. Her proven thesis was to have lightbulbs illuminate from ionic charges sent through the air. Some thought it was the magical alchemy of David Copperfield. Sylvania, Westinghouse, and other lightbulb manufacturers knew otherwise and immediately understood the threat. Not surprisingly, General Electric bought the patent (for over ten million bucks) and stashed it in the basement of Rockefeller Center while they continue to sell incandescent, screw-in filament bulbs in every hardware store in America.

This experience with big business soured Melody. *Sad,* she thought, *to devote all that creative energy and imagination to improve the world and have it gobbled by greed.* Admittedly, she did pocket ten million bucks, so let's not put her on a par with Mother Teresa—not quite yet. However, it did demonstrate to her that the money motive could get in the way of true invention.

"What we must do is think outside the box. Why? Just because we can," she recently told a Mensa Society gathering in the Manila, Philippines. "If we prethink a profitable business plan, the idea will automatically be compromised. If anything, our motive should be to release the human spirit . . . and shock the world that anything is possible."

This speaking tour of Mensa had proven to be a thrill for Melody Gerhardt. For one thing, she did not have to talk down to her audience. Most of her fellow members were similarly afflicted with the ability to connect with short-term commercial interests. For her listening audience, it was almost always energizing to think of bigger implications.

Case in point: Rowell Wang. He is the brilliant warden of the state prison and a curious soul who has always wished to inspire his depressed prisoners to "break the stereotype and dream bigger dreams."

Over a late-night cup of coffee, he presented this very challenge to Melody Gerhardt and challenged the woman to use her creative/choreographic/artistic sensibilities to "change the way the world thinks about 'the incarcerated.'"

I am assuming you may have seen the video called "Thriller in Prison." As a nonmember of the Mensa Society, I innocently judge it amazing. Fifteen hundred hard-core, orange-attired prisoners dance in lockstep and inspire every viewer to smile as they zombie-walk to Michael Jackson's big hit. It's weirdly awe-inspiring. How could anyone think of this? It is still ranked in the top ten of all YouTube hits in the past decade. (At its height, it had three hundred thousand hits a week. To date, more than fifty million people have viewed it.)

On the heels of this, the rate of prisoners' pride and reentry into society has increased by 32 percent. Recidivism has decreased by 40 percent. Tourism to Singapore has increased by 82 percent.

However, Melody Gerhardt has learned that she can no longer be a hostage to specifics. Perhaps that's why she has recently been a key player in a new movement she is tentatively calling Arab Spring. Someday, it may amount to something. As she recently admitted, "It will certainly be a departure from the status quo, and that in itself is potentially healthy."

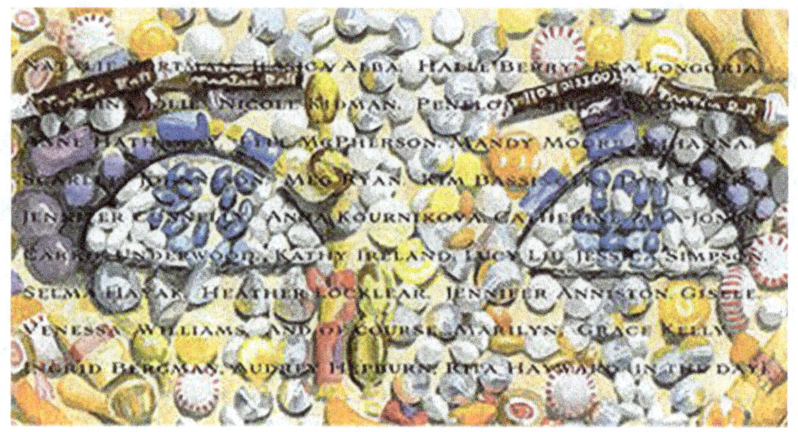

Eye Candy
Watercolor
33 × 22
2009

Eye Candy

As a cum laude communications graduate of Syracuse University, Elinore Banfield always resented the term *eye candy*. However, as a dead ringer for Rachel McAdams, it was inevitable that some people would call her that, if only behind her back.

In a profession that relies, to a large degree, on visual impact, it was always difficult to ignore her physical assets. Some would say she was gifted with good genes—bright blue eyes, flawless skin, luscious lips, and natural blond hair. However, as she often reminded people, she had chosen broadcast journalism because of a burning desire to keep people informed and to unearth the sometimes ugly truth below the surface. In order to foster this image, Elinore normally dressed in plain-Jane outfits (neutral earth tones) and usually donned horn-rimmed glasses, which were strictly for cosmetic reasons. However, this simply communicated a naughty-librarian persona to her viewing audience. Such was the indefinable magnetic appeal of Elinore Banfield.

The commercials for her first gig as a news anchor on WISH-TV in Indianapolis played upon her visual appeal. She had been a local reporter on this popular TV station for the past eighteen months and had toiled the vineyards of council meetings and car crashes, but she had just been promoted to the 11:00 p.m. co-news anchor slot.

The WISH-TV campaign to promote her ascent was frankly suggestive. It showcased Elinore in many locales—laughing, interrogating, with glasses, without glasses—and was summed up with the line, "Your wish has come true. Meet Ellie eye to eye tonight at 11:00 p.m. on WISH-TV . . . where the news gets personal." The video ended with an outtake of Elinore Banfield winking at the camera.

Of course, she was livid. For starters, she never liked being called Ellie—as if she was a high-school prom date. More damaging, she hated the prurient appeal of the message and the wink at the end. However, as a twenty-five-year-old news anchor, she did not have that much leverage. She did succeed in having the announcer rename her Elinore and substitute a last frame wave at the camera, replacing the wink. However, these were Pyrrhic victories. The gestalt of the commercial remained the same—a sexy encounter with the new face on WISH-TV.

Almost immediately, ratings soared. Within three months, the newscast had become no. 1 in its time slot. Admittedly, it was helped by the lead-in to *Late Show with David Letterman*, but that had been the case for the past twelve months. The only true variable was the addition of the beautiful anchor to the 11:00 p.m. telecast.

Not surprisingly, the people at CBS corporate in New York began to notice and began to see a light at the end of the tunnel for the perennial, also-ran status of the *CBS Morning News*. It had lagged behind the *Today* show for decades and now even trailed *Good Morning America* on ABC. The fact that it was called Morning News was one of the problems. At 7:00 a.m., no one but the old CBS brass wanted a serious news problem. Such a positioning was akin to studying Latin or practicing the oboe before breakfast. No, this was a time for light banter, celeb interviews, and a smattering of news headlines always handled in a lighthearted way.

Add to this the fact that CBS had hosted the show with a fifty-nine-year-old white male news veteran who had roots in the first Bush administration. Well, you can imagine the disconnection.

So Elinore was tapped along with Harvey Levin, the man who made TMZ famous. Unlike all the other New York–based morning shows, this new program would be based in Los Angeles. Given the time difference, it would exude a late late–night personality (still happening) rather than a bleary-eyed, no-one-is-awake, before-sunrise approach.

It would be called *CBS Wake-Up Call*.

The kickoff commercials said it all. Ten-second spots barraged the networks with the message, "Wake up to this!" It was followed by a smiling Elinore Banfield (occasionally alternated with Harvey Levin just to avoid criticism). And then quick-cut stills of Kim Kardashian, Ryan Gosling, Arnold Schwarzenegger, Paris Hilton, a few political/government figures, Kobe Bryant, Mark Zuckerberg, Marcia Clark, Halle Berry, Pee-wee Herman, Kathy Ireland, and President Barrack Obama, then a slow burn on Elinore's face, with the voice-over, "Waking up has never been so exciting!"

Unless you sleep until 10:00 a.m., you know the results. *Wake Up* is now the no. 1 morning show. Elinore's initial interview with Charlie Sheen snowballed into a YouTube phenomenon. (He actually propositioned her in front of a live audience.) If you saw the premiere, you saw him dig into the brandy snifter of assorted candies and suggest that she might actually "taste better."

Few people remember that Elinore Banfield actually earned an Emmy for her searing interview three weeks later with Justice Antonin Scalia, when he admitted a bias toward "white-colored" candy as he reached into the jar. But it was good—virtually unnoticed, but good. Meanwhile, the early-morning candy continues to be consumed by millions of unfulfilled, fantasizing, forever-fickle-for-escape viewers.

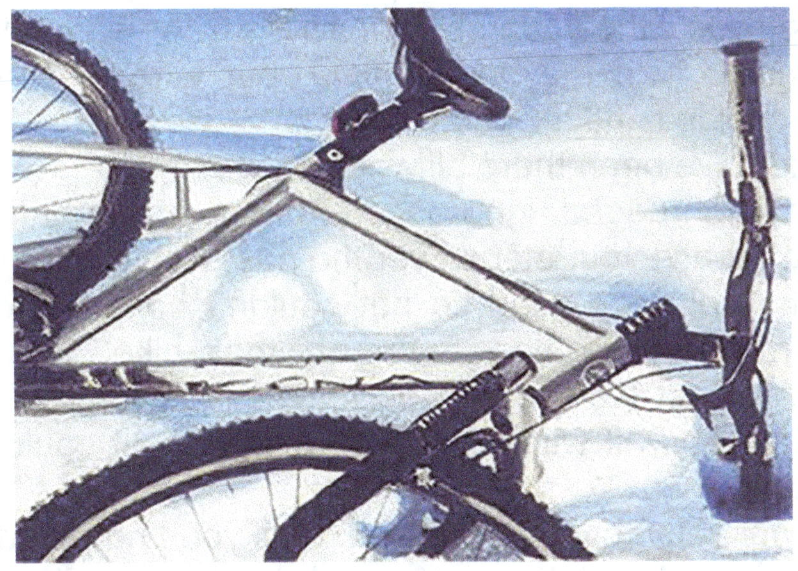

Snow Bike

"Mitchell, for the umpteenth time, put your bicycle in the garage."

"Mitchell, please pick up your dirty clothes and put them in the hamper."

"Mitchell, how many times do I need to tell you? Bring your damn plates to the kitchen sink."

Despite Sophie Byrne's constant reminders to her son, this single mom's admonitions never seemed to register to young Mitchell. Perhaps it would be charitable to call him a young man who loved to live very much in the moment. More likely, he was simply a sloppy, forgetful twelve-year-old kid who left his belongings anywhere and everywhere he went.

In most cases, his trail of debris created no real harm. However, the incident of the missing bike did prove vexing to Mitchell Byrne.

"I think someone must have stolen it," he explained to his mother one cold December day. Of course, most December days in their Montana home were cold. More than a few were gray. And shortly after Thanksgiving, the vast majority of those short days were snowy.

"When did you last have it?" a frustrated Sophie Byrne asked her son.

"That's the thing," the young boy answered. "At least a week ago, I remember riding it in the soccer field, but when I checked back yesterday, I couldn't find it."

"So it could have been there all week?"

Mitchell just shrugged ignorance, further exacerbating Sophie. "You have to retrace your steps over the past week," Mom scolded.

The boy had already done so but couldn't honestly recollect the exact last moment he had been on that bike. So much had happened this past week—classes, basketball practice, visits with friends, and on-and-off winter snowstorms. He just couldn't pinpoint his last bike trip.

"Well, I'm *not* getting you a new one, until you find that damn bike," his mom finally and angrily pronounced, hoping that it might jog his memory or at least send a signal that replacement money didn't grow on trees, especially around Christmastime.

By the end of January, the bike had not been found. It was still MIA through February and March and the first several weeks of April. By tax time, however, the temperature had begun to rise, the big Montana sky had began to showcase the sun, and right on schedule, the snow had begun to melt. All that was the expected rite of spring. What was not expected was the call from a Mr. Martin Carlyle, the widowed farmer who owned a ranch seven miles from the Byrne home.

"Did your son have a silver-colored Kona bike?" he asked Sophie Byrne, who had answered the phone. The man had explained that his daughter was in her eighth-grade class at Montana Mountain junior high school with Mitchell, and she seemed to remember that her fellow classmate once had that once-shiny bicycle.

"Yes, that sounds like my son's bike. We'll be there in twenty minutes," Mom replied. Fuming at his forgetfulness, she piled her young son in the pickup to deal with his comeuppance

"You remember riding it out here," Mom accused.

"Never," the kid answered emphatically, partly to reinforce that he had no interest whatsoever in young Brittany Carlyle, who had walked the field with her dad and discovered the bike. Ever since Mitchell had arrived on the farm, she had been coyly smiling at her classmate.

"Did you have a lock?" Mr. Carlyle asked, breaking the uncomfortable silence.

"Never felt we needed it in these parts. Why else do we call it God's country?" Mrs. Byrne replied.

"Hey, welcome to the twenty-first century," Mr. Carlyle laughed and loaded the bike in Mrs. Byrne's pickup. "There are plenty of bored roughnecks in this area who might have stolen your bike and taken it on some joyride. Of course, none of them will ever admit it. Point is, maybe your son is not at fault in this particular case."

At that precise moment, Mitchell Byrne felt like jumping over the truck bed and embracing this stranger with a thank-you hug.

On the way home, Mrs. Byrne didn't quite apologize. However, she did smile at her son and told him how proud she was of the fact that the snafu was an innocent mistake—not of his making, not his mistake. She also vowed to buy him a topflight bicycle lock the very next day.

After about ten minutes, Mrs. Byrne tried to break the ice again. "Cute girl, Brittany. Any interest?"

Mitchell just looked out the rearview window of his retrieved bike and shook his head. "No way. Mr. Carlyle is nice, though."

The observation had already occurred to her. A thank-you note would be nice. A thank-you dinner would be even nicer. At the thought of this prospect, the lonely mother smiled again. After a few more seconds, she looked over to Mitchell and actually admitted that it was not his fault.

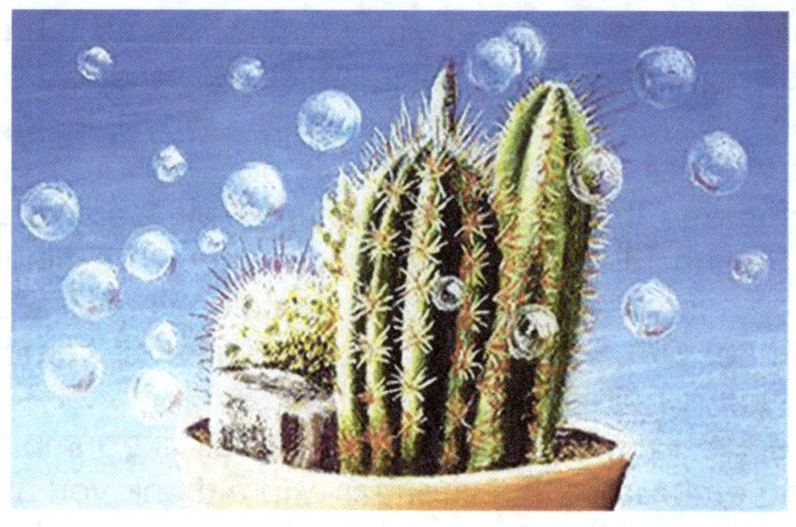

Kids Were No Longer Welcomed

To be sure, Franco Rodriguez had outlived the once-friendly family neighborhood in the southwest corner of Mesa, Arizona.

The milestone wasn't just a function of years. Yes, Mr. Rodriguez, as the students once called him, was now eighty-three years old. However, the reclusive nature of the man had less to do with longevity and more to do with a string of unfortunate circumstances. His wife had passed thirty years ago with a bout of leukemia, and the man had neither the heart nor the energy to reengage. His sole daughter had been killed twenty years ago in a drunk-driving accident.

Most likely, that was enough to take the starch out of the once-optimistic man. However, the events at Mesa Plains Grade School added fuel to the fire. Here, Franco Rodriquez had been the principal for the last thirteen years of his tenure. It had been a glorious career of academic achievement until 1992, when a sixth-grade student named Alison Markley had an epileptic attack and died in the classroom.

Some blamed the ER unit for being late. More blame went to the school, which, according to the police, had waited seven crucial minutes before calling 911. Evidently, there was no epilepsy procedure in place. There was a lawsuit. Despite Principal Rodriquez's protests, the district paid a civil penalty of one million dollars. On the day of the verdict, Franco Rodriquez offered his resignation. It was accepted even before the superintendent reached for the envelope.

Until yesterday, that was the last time Franco had any congress with his neighbors. As a matter of fact, every signal sent discouraged visitors. He had installed a security system and placed signs in the front of the yard every twenty yards that warned passersby not to trespass. He had an invisible fence with a yappy mastiff dog, which barked at every loving couple walking through the street. Just as daunting, he had constructed a labyrinth of saguaro cacti in every corner of his front yard to discourage any child to play on his property.

"Mr. Rodriquez, I am sorry to call you, but I desperately need your help," his neighbor Dominique Washington cried at 10:00 a.m. this morning. "My son has a 105-degree fever, and I need to get him to the emergency ward. The doctor suggests I should come along with him. My parents are out of town. My friends are all at work. I am calling as a last resort. Could you possibly watch my four-year-old daughter, Chloe, for a few hours . . . please?"

After a few seconds pause, Franco agreed to meet the mother at the curb.

"Here are some toys and playthings," the woman offered, holding out a bag. And then she handed over young Chloe to the old man.

"Don't worry." He nodded. "I used to know how to do this." Nonetheless, the little girl was clearly frightened and started crying as they headed into the house.

"I'll call as soon as I know what's up," the mother said, and she ran into the house and soon rushed her son to the hospital.

To Franco's surprise, his mastiff, Hugo, was the icebreaker. The large taffy-colored beast slinked across the floor and bowed to the young girl. Then the dog turned on her back, and Chloe rubbed her tummy.

"You know how to make grilled-cheese sandwiches?" the young girl then asked. The old man opened up some Kraft Singles and Wonder Bread, and he remembered how he used to make the gooey concoction for his own daughter twenty years ago.

He then opened up Chloe's bag of tricks and toys. First, there was a short game of chutes and ladders. Then he reached for the bottle of blow bubbles. "Let's do these in the backyard," the old man suggested.

Chloe followed, and they soon blew bubbles into the cacti and watched the fragile soapy circles explode into the needles. *Pop! Pop! Boom! Ping!* The twosome soon turned it into a game.

"Betcha I can explode more bubbles than you can," Mr. Rodriguez teased.

"No way," the little girl answered. And the aerial attack of bubbles ensued for at least forty minutes.

The fun was only interrupted by the unaccustomed ring of the telephone in the kitchen. Mr. Rodriguez held up a finger to pause the contest and was followed by young Chloe into the kitchen past the sleeping Hugo.

"I'm going to be here at least until midnight," Mrs. Washington apologized. Before waiting for a reply, she added, "But I can have my friend Laura pick up Chloe in about two hours."

"Well, yes . . . but . . ." Mr. Rodriguez fumbled. Then little Chloe interrupted and asked if the call was from her mom. Franco nodded and handed her the phone. The little girl listened and responded, "Uh-huh. Uh-huh. But we're having fun. Can't I stay here until you get home? Please. Please. Please."

After quick assurances from Mr. Rodriquez, the old man and the little girl played until sunset, enjoyed mac and cheese, and watched a few cartoons until the little girl fell asleep on the sofa next to the lonely, once-lively man.

With the ring of the doorbell, Mr. Rodriguez jumped to his feet and greeted his neighbor.

"How's the boy?"

"Better. How's my girl?"

"Wonderful."

Without a further word, the old man walked over to his sofa and gently reached for little Chloe. He then offered to carry her across the street to the Washington home. As he dodged the cacti, he did make a mental promise to trim those dangerous needles or at least get more bubble blows for the next time his new friend would visit.

"I have to go to the hospital again first thing in the morning," Mrs. Washington admitted.

"I still have her toys," the old man admitted. "And I still have her blow bubbles." Franco Rodriguez laughed and dodged the cacti back home, anticipating tomorrow for the first time in so many years.

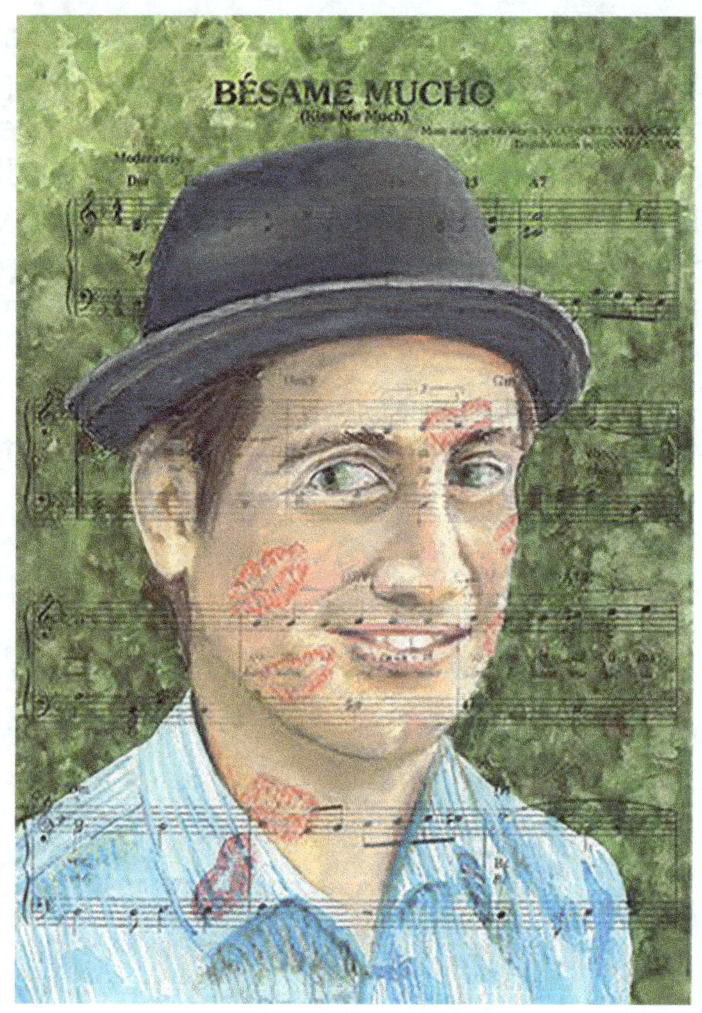

Besame Mucho
Watercolor and pastel
18 × 24
2012

Besame Mucho

He did not resemble Clark Gable of the 1930s, nor was he a retro throwback to Paul Newman of the 1960s. However, all the Brad Pitts, Ryan Goslings, and Johnny Depps of the new millennium could not hold a candle to Philip Devereux—at least in terms of his ability to attract women's kisses.

To be honest, his secret was so damn simple: he not only loved women, he liked them.

He liked the way they thought, laughed, worked, giggled at kids' innocence, abhorred pomposity, and fought back tears in movies. He admired women's ability to instinctively cook, dance to almost any kind of music, love animals (not just dogs), hate almost every injustice, and have deep discussions of a pointless nature on any subject. He was forever intrigued by their public affection, innate mystery, less-than-linear creativity, and the always-adventurous music in their soul.

Women, in return, not only loved Philip Devereux. They liked him.

He talked with them. He asked their honest opinions. Most importantly, he listened to their hearts without surreptitiously stealing glances at his wristwatch.

In some ways, Philip's job made this connection possible. Or perhaps it was the other way around. As the head producer of *Chelsea Lately*, one of his responsibilities was to warm up the guests, make them completely comfortable with the interview show, and instill them with the confidence that they will be stunningly wonderful in front of a national audience. As Chelsea Handler recently admitted in *Vanity Fair* magazine, "No single person is better at preparing my guests for their televised roller-coaster ride than Philip Devereux." According to the reporter, Ms. Handler then smooched an "air kiss" in the direction of the set, with the message "All women love you, Philip."

Given his success on the program, it was something of a bombshell when Devereux announced that he would be leaving the popular talk show. Unlike most departures that merit a five-minute farewell, Chelsea Handler decided to devote a complete show to the man's contribution and invited seven women who willingly admitted that all men should be as sensitive as Philip Devereux. One by one, Salma Hayek, Jessica Simpson, Faith Hill, Wanda Sykes, Margaret Cho, Cameron Diaz, and Alex Wagner complimented the man and planted an indelible kiss on his face. After a few lip-locks, the studio band improvised the conga line of kissers and accompanied the sequential affection with the Latino hit "Besame Mucho." As they say in showbiz, it was one of those unscripted magic moments.

By the next morning, the kiss photo was distributed on all the tabloids, the *Hollywood Reporter* and the *New York Post.*

Over the next several weeks, the distribution of the picture became more widespread, and ensuing stories of Philip's unique ability to relate to women became more legendary. Given his sudden popularity and the pull of the picture, it also became the poster for Philip's new talk show on OWN, Oprah Winfrey's television network.

"I'm so happy to have this new program and celebrate the fact that understanding, honoring, appreciating . . . and just getting a real kick out of women is in everyone's interest in 2013," Oprah said when she announced the premiere of the new show. Then she pointed to the wings and continued, "No one captures that better than my friend, Philip Devereux." The man entered from the left stage and blew a kiss to the audience. Then Oprah planted an indelible lip imprint on his right cheek. Not surprisingly, he left the image on his cheek throughout the program as he has done on every succeeding show from a parade of other female guests, including a very gracious Chelsea Handler. After all, with a show called *Besame Mucho*, it only makes sense to play off the title with every shot of the host.

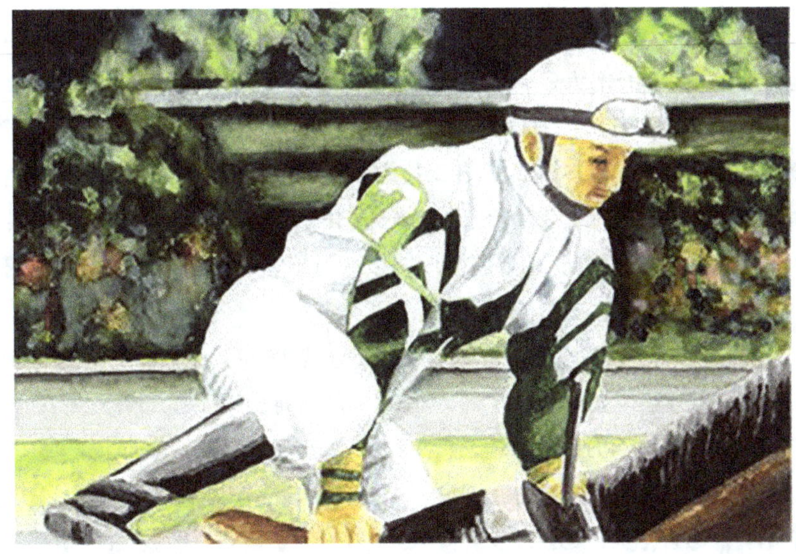

The Not-So-Sure Thing

For the past three decades, no racehorse has won the Triple Crown. The last one was Secretariat, who set a course record, winning by thirty-one lengths and a full six seconds faster than the runner-up. That was in 1973. Since then, there were eight worthy double victors in the mile-long Kentucky Derby and the mile-and-quarter Preakness, but every potential immortal faltered on the grueling mile-and-half Belmont track.

This particular year was supposed to be different. Many casual race fans fell in love with the horse's name—Smarty Jones. True racing aficionados gushed at the champion's record. The three-year-old had never been beaten—he won eight different races at eight lengths. For weeks, the ballyhoo about this racehorse extended beyond the sports pages. He became the great hope for a once-in-a-generation miracle, and his story was featured on front pages, TVs, and watercooler talks around the nation.

I had never attended the Belmont Stakes, but something said this was the year to be there. In part, I wanted to witness history. I admit to another part, the shot at making a quick payoff on the horse everyone called a sure thing.

On the way to the event, I battled the bumper-to-bumper traffic on the Van Wyck Expressway to arrive at the racetrack a few hours before the main event. Immediately, I realized I was underdressed. Men in blue blazers and bow ties were holding court on the second floor of the grandstand. Women wearing floppy, flowerful straw hats were holding champagne flutes. No kids. This was an adult event, attended by rather upscale adults.

A somber announcement interrupted the country-clubbish chitchat and the celebratory pour of Moët. At 1:25 p.m., the racecourse announcer departed from declaring the scratches for Race no. 3 and said, "Ladies and Gentlemen, we have just learned that our fortieth president of the United States, Ronald Wilson Reagan, has passed away. As a show of respect, let us pause for a minute of silence."

A slight pause did ensue. Some people made a sign of the cross across their chests. More shook hands with their friends and reclinked their glasses for the legendary race to come. After all, Ronald Reagan was then, Smarty Jones was now.

After a few small bets on the midraces, I decided to put $100 on the big race. I also decided to go to the paddock to see the sterling stallion and feel encouraged about my wager. I was. What a specimen! When the Canadian jockey Stewart Elliott mounted America's favorite horse, I instinctively knew I was about to see history unfold.

Admittedly, it was a meager 1–5 wager, meaning that it would only make forty bucks on my wager—enough to pay for my parking and cocktails, enough to compensate for my earlier losses. However, I instinctively knew that a May 14 Belmont receipt of the Triple Crown victory would eventually be worth thousands.

"And . . . they're off," the track announcer broadcasted to the history-inclined crowd. There was a definite buzz, which became a deafening roar within one minute. As expected, Smarty Jones led throughout the race. Then there was the last eighth. At this pole, the amazing, legendary champion began to slowly fade, and yet, he continued his quest. Even until the last hundred yards, history was in the making. And then, the legend was gassed. A 36–1 shot named Birdstone surpassed him at the wire by one length and dashed the dreams of 120,000 spectators.

It went from a thunderous roar to stunned silence in one minute. It was more dramatic and lasted longer than the announcement that Ronald Reagan had died. For so many, it had the element of surprise. For many like me, it was sad.

Someday, I will perhaps see the amazing Mets again win the World Series. I will perhaps see NY Jets win another Super Bowl since the unexpected no. 3. Hey, maybe I will someday enjoy the Chicago Cubs win their first World Series in eighty years. But I had my one chance to see sports history made. And I know how wrong it all can go.

PS: By the way, I still hold on to that losing ticket on the Belmont race no. 8 on May 4, 1973. If this string of disrupted Triple Crown winners continues, my losing ticket on this "one sure thing" may end up being worth something someday.

Firemen, Nurses, Police Officers, Ski patrol,
Guidance Counselors, Doctors, Ambulance corps,
Lawyers (sometimes), Secret Service, Priests,
Conservationists, Friends, Medical Researchers,
Rehabbers, Nutritionists, Lasolt, Family members,
FBI agents, Dogs, Therapists, Snowplowers,
Coaches, Spouses, Donors, Peace Keepers,
Kittens, Farmers, Security Guards, Referees,
Condoms, Hurricane Analysts, Beach Patrol.
Volunteers, Crossing Guards, Flight Attendants.

Life Savers
Watercolor and pastel
29 × 18
2004

A Lifesaver

There are signs along the Tappan Zee Bridge that read, "Life is worth living."

Presumably, they were placed there to discourage troubled souls from leaping into the waters of the Hudson River.

Perhaps Clarence Adderly had not observed the posted messages. More likely, he chose to ignore them.

I was following behind Mr. Adderly when his Chevy Malibu slowed to a stop in the right lane. "Damn, I can't believe it," I angrily reacted, frustrated that I would now be delayed on this rush-hour bridge because of a stalled car. When I saw him leave his Malibu and start climbing up the ledge, it became clear to me that the problem was not a disabled vehicle. It was a disabled human spirit.

"Don't jump!" I screamed out to the man as I raced from my blocked car. Don't canonize me; I am not a natural Good Samaritan, just a sixty-year-old salesman trying to move through life. But I couldn't just sit there and watch a suicide in the making.

"Go away," Adderly called back to me as he held on to the heavy wire cable.

I took this as a good sign. Maybe the presence of an audience would be enough to discourage the act. As I inched forward, I prayed that some other driver would be calling 911. *If I could only keep him from offing himself until the professionals arrived.*

"Give me one reason not to jump," the man said, staring at the abyss.

A litany of rationales flooded my brain—*because people love you, because tomorrow will be better, because it's selfish*. None of them felt adequate.

"Can't think of one can you?" Adderly taunted me.

"Because it'll hurt," I said.

"I already hurt."

"Exactly. So this is not a good way to go," I countered.

For the next five or six minutes, we discussed alternative suicide methods—a painless overdose, an instant gunshot, numbing carbon monoxide. By now, the impatient New York drivers were blaring their horns, unwittingly egging him on. *Where the hell are the trained police psychologists?* I thought. Looking at the now-chockablock traffic, I assumed it was impossible to get through the gridlock.

We continued talking. For the next ten minutes or so, we discussed the pros and cons of each means and the extra pain of this particular style of suicide. It seemed to be sinking in.

"You think it's really cold?" the man said, peering over the ledge.

"Icy. And hard," I said. "And it's a long, long way down."

After an excruciating pause, Adderly heaved a huge frustrated sigh and eased himself down off the bridge.

"You've given me some things to think about," the man told me and stumbled toward his car.

"Not so fast," I said as gently as I could. "You should really talk to someone."

"There's no one."

"There's me," I said and scribbled my home phone number on a business card. I gave it to Adderly, whose pores exuded that once-and-always familiar smell of liquor.

He never called. Hopefully, he awoke from his stupor the next morning, looked himself in the mirror, and got help. Given his pain, it's not inconceivable that he eventually took the easier route—the painkiller overdose. I never found out. At least it didn't happen on my watch.

You can't save yourself unless you want to, I told myself. I looked at my unopened bottle of Johnnie Walker across my desk. Given the ordeal, I admit to being more tempted to take a sip than I had in the past seven years and four months. Instead, I opened up the silver foil of the package and popped a bright-red Life Saver in my mouth. It was benignly sweet. However, I do confess to being tempted by the smoky, forbidden, dangerous allure of the Black Jack that beckoned like a siren next to my computer screen. *One day at a time*, I reminded myself.

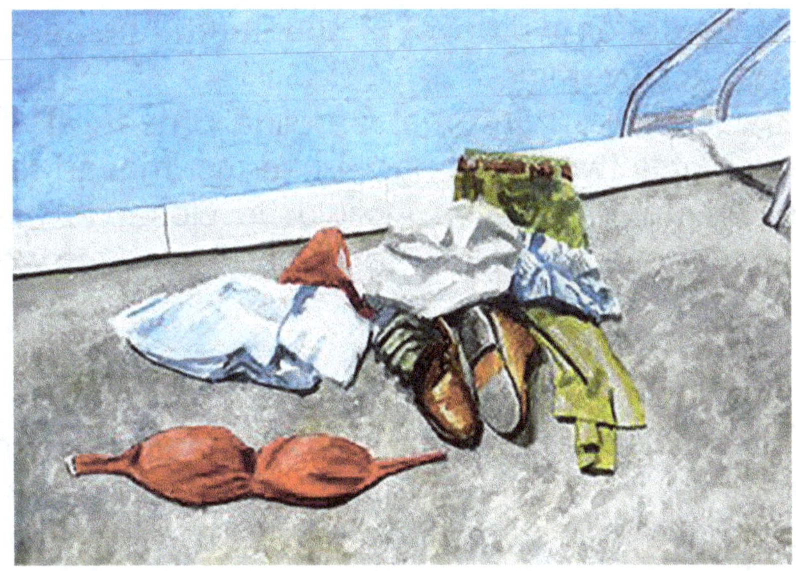

The Skinny-Dippers

It was a completely unexpected, uninvited admission from Mrs. Carolina Bateau, the most attractive fortyish woman in Greenwich, Connecticut, at our kid's high school preprom party.

She clinked her glass to mine and then winked. "Given the damn heat, the only thing that relieves it is to skinny-dip around one p.m. . . . don't you agree?"

I wish there was a camera on me, because I am certain there were three reactions: (1) a head jolt of at least twelve inches; (2) a goofy finger pointed in the middle of my chest as if to suggest, "Are you really talking to me?"; (3) a swivel-headed look 180 degrees to my left and then to my right to reassure myself that no one was actually listening.

"Yes, yes, yes . . . it has been damn hot, but all I have is a shower." *How stupid did I just sound?* "You have a pool?" I asked as if it were a legit proposition.

She sipped her glass of wine next to me and looked around at our high school kids in tuxedoes and pastel dresses. "I don't imagine any of them will be home for forty-eight hours," Mrs. Bateau again clinked my glass.

"So what do we do for two days?" I countered, then smiled proudly as if it really was a clever line.

Let's backtrack a little. I first met Carolina Bateau at one of those back-to-school nights two years ago. I had just moved to Greenwich after a rather painful divorce so I could be closer to the kids' new school. On a coffee break, I still remember her first words to me, "New in town?"

"Two weeks new," I answered.

"Don't believe everything you've heard about me," she said. Then she took a bite of her cookie, put the other half in my mouth, and walked away. I felt as if I were in that movie *Body Heat* with a horny Kathleen Turner. Fact is, I had not heard anything about Carolina Bateau, but I have since. She is the very successful, very wealthy writer of erotica, who lives on Round Hill Road. She is "loosely" married to some muckety-muck on Wall Street who travels two hundred days a year.

I, on the other hand, am still a financially strapped apartment dweller who has a modest insurance business. Oh, and in the interest of full disclosure, I have never been one to chase "tail" as my seventeen-year-old son and his friends call it. However, when it falls in my lap . . .

When the prom kids boarded the private vans, we all waved good-bye, fully understanding that many of them were going to a cottage in Kingston at midnight after the dance for who knows what? OK, we all know what. As I looked at the well-wishing parents, I couldn't help but notice Carolina toasting them bon voyage and then winking at me.

By the time I went to bed that night, I knew at least some of what would happen tomorrow. By 1:00 p.m., I was driving on Round Hill Road, feeling a bit dorky for being so punctual. Even so, it was stupid to just waste time driving to and fro. So I walked up to the doorbell and pushed it. No answer. I then walked into the backyard. By the pool steps, I could see a red bikini and a towel. Within a few seconds, Carolina popped her head out of the deep end.

"You look hot," she volunteered.

"Well, as you said yesterday, at this time of day, the sun does beat down," I answered, idiotically ignoring her double entendre.

"Join me," she answered, getting right to the point.

"I didn't bring a swimsuit." *Wow*, I mentally kicked myself, *I am really bad and so damn out of practice at this.*

"Join me," she repeated.

I stripped down and laid my clothes next to hers, doing my best to seem nonchalant in this striptease. However, having been a solo guy since my divorce, I am sure I looked as nervous as a seventeen-year-old. Without hesitation, I jumped in the pool and sidled up next to Mrs. Bateau.

"Whoa, down, boy," she giggled.

I am going to be quite honest with you. I don't know where I thought this escapade would lead. Yes, I do. Sex. Given the woman's teases, I couldn't help but think that. At least a one-afternoon stand? As a matter of fact, I actually thought it would probably be better that way.

"We should really get to the point," Carolina advised. "Because I think my husband may be returning home soon."

"No! Stop! Your husband is coming?"

"He should be on his way. But you know flights these days, they're usually late," she laughed and then reached to touch me. It was like the first chapters of one of her dangerous, erotic novels (OK, I did read a few just for research).

I think I jumped out of the pool like a cat that just experienced an electrical shock. Within about ten seconds, I was fully dressed. It's not that I am chicken about a fight, but I'd rather not have a scuffle about a woman who has lured me into harm's way for her own playacting amusement.

"You should come back when my husband is not here," she teased. Without comment, I jogged to my Toyota and sped away, passing a limo pulling into the driveway in the opposite direction.

The next day, my seventeen-year-old son arrived home after his extended prom.

"How was it?" I asked, instinctively knowing not to pry too directly.

"Cool, the dance was just OK, but the cottage in Kingston was spectacular. Even had a pool!"

I didn't want to ask if he had a swimming suit in his overnight bag. Why bring an unflattering, forever-unspoken comparison to my own encounter?

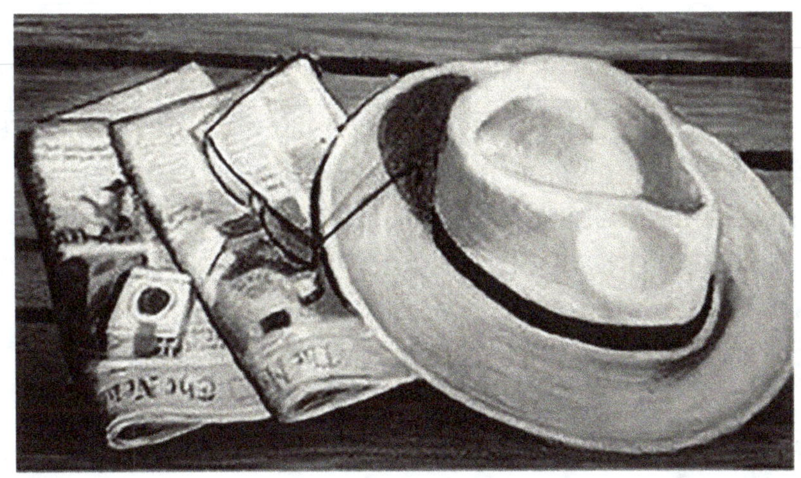

Mr. Lucky

In the late 1950s, Mark Bollinger would sheepishly admit to his cohorts that he lived "a charmed life." How else could you explain the fact that this C+ Mizzou grad could hobnob every day with the Princeton, Harvard, Yale captains of industry and tell them exactly how to spend their advertising dollars?

Part of his success was an innate gift of the gab and an ingrained belief that no one automatically deserved a higher station than others. His Midwestern parents had instilled this confidence in him as a young man. However, Bollinger had more than kept his end of the bargain, and he was a quintessential prototypal *Mad Man*, long before the hit series. Even in his early days at the McKinney-Ross agency, he dressed in Paul Stuart attire, learned how to appreciate Cutty and Lucky Strikes, and was an avid daily reader of the *New York Times*—all the things that his bosses and Ivy League clients did. In addition, he had the "central casting" personal life—a gorgeous blond wife called Kathy, two kids, a cocker spaniel, and a split-level home in tony Pelham Manor.

Bollinger's actual contributions to the creativity of advertising were minimal.

Within the bowels of the agency, he had copywriters and art directors for that fulfillment task. This is not to minimize his role within the walls of McKinney-Ross. Fact is, most of the creative staff courted the tanned, trim executive. They wanted his blessing since no one could sell a campaign to clients like David Rockefeller, Henry Ford, or the IBM folks like Mark Bollinger. Perhaps that's one reason he was promoted to president of the agency in 1966.

"McKinney-Ross promotes rising star to the corner office," screamed *Ad Age*.

"Meet the new king of Madison Avenue," the *New York Times* proclaimed.

"Advertising has a new leader," the *Wall Street Journal* understated.

However, shortly after his much-ballyhooed elevation, Mr. Bollinger's luck suddenly began to change. Put more accurately, the advertising industry suddenly began to change. The gentlemanly, account-driven, old-boys network became increasingly less relevant. What took its place? A rise in counterculture as evidenced by underdog campaigns such as VW "Lemon," Avis "We Try Harder," and "The Pepsi Generation."

These efforts became the new darlings of the fickle trade press and pushed McKinney-Ross to the back pages, usually with a harshly critical news slant. As a result, several of the more creatively oriented accounts began to exit McKinney-Ross. Alka-Seltzer deserted to embark on a "Spicy Meatball" campaign. Foster Grant found a new home for more creative advertising, as did Clairol and Black & Decker. Of course, it wasn't a complete exodus. Stalwart clients like AT&T, Ford, and IBM stayed with the agency with the promise from the beleaguered CEO that within the agency, things would soon change.

In 1972, the fallen golden boy tried to adjust to the creative revolution by hiring three different copy gurus in the space of five years. Some unflattering trade newspapers even compared him to George Steinbrenner for his penchant to "play musical chairs with creative executives."

Fortunately, there was one other trend that had just begun to emerge in the agency business. Bollinger had learned it from his Ivy League banking friends. Their advice: "Think mergers. Think acquisitions. Reverse acquisitions. IPOs. Golden parachutes. It can be good for everyone, including your employees."

So Mr. Lucky began shopping. The overture from the British grocery-cart manufacturer took Bollinger by surprise—mostly because it was so damn lucrative. It would mean millions for several of his trusted lieutenants and tens of millions for him. Never one to stew over the fine print, it took Bollinger about twenty-two days to cement the agreement.

Upon the completion of the deal, Mark Bollinger and Martin Sorrell went to Ben Benson's steak house and privately celebrated the largest acquisition ever made in the agency business.

"Lucky?" Sorrell asked and extended the so-named cigarette to Bollinger.

"I don't know any other word for it," the man admitted, ignited the gift with his Zippo, took a drag, and then toasted the new owner of McKinney-Ross.

That night, at the New York Athletic Club, Bollinger would again hobnob with the heads of corporations, who still had to slog it out every single day—whether they actually wanted to or not. As America's richest unemployed executive shared a dinner with his cohorts, Mr. Lucky quietly reminded himself that he indeed did lead a "charmed life."

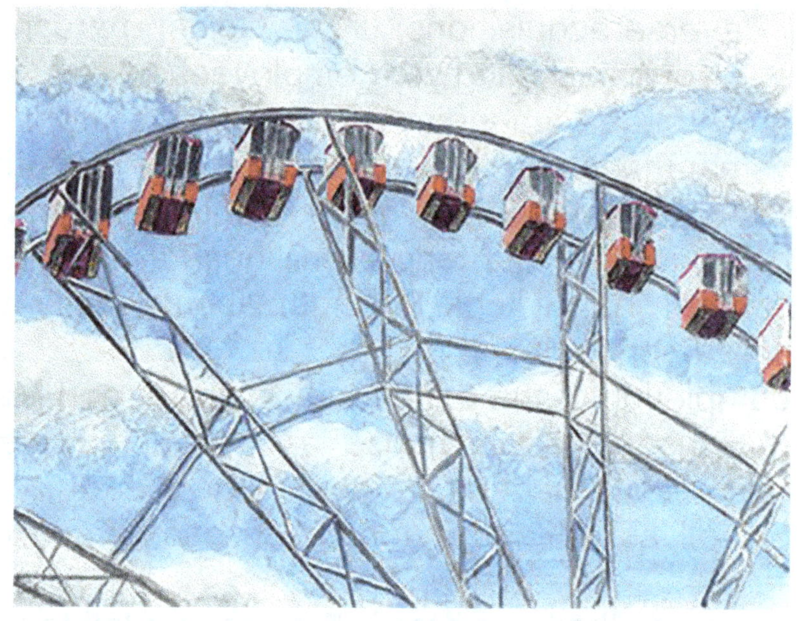

The First Time

Angela Avelos squinted at the contraption in the sky and immediately felt dizzy. Admittedly, she was not the bravest girl in the world. After all, she was only twelve, barely five feet tall, and as such, often felt overpowered and dwarfed by the big, wide world.

"This is the biggest, greatest Ferris wheel in all of America," her older cousin Michelle announced as they approached the machine.

"Yikes," Angela immediately responded when she reached the base of the attraction that seemed to reach into the clouds. To Angela, it looked like something from a sci-fi movie—a blazing, blaring, white-hot confusion of metal struts that blurred into the blinding sun.

It was the first real hiccup on this weekend trip to Angela's aunt's house. The family had made the six-hour drive from Little Rock for the simple reason of reconnecting with kin. "I don't even know Michelle," Angela complained in the backseat of the car.

"So that's a good reason to take this trip," Mom answered. "It's just a good way to become acquainted with your blood relatives."

The first twenty-four hours went smoothly. The grown-ups all swapped stories about growing up, and the two young girls compared notes about movies, Facebook, and of course, local boys.

"If we go to the Texas State Fair tomorrow, a couple of young cowboys might be there to squire us around. I like Brad, but Troy's cute too, and he expressed a hankerin' to tag along to meet my Arkansas cousin. You game?" Michelle asked.

"Let me see his picture on Facebook," Angela requested. When she discovered that he didn't have too many pimples, she agreed to the arranged introduction.

It was to happen at the base of the Texas Star after a morning of shows, pig races, and every imaginable kind of fried food.

"I want to show Angela the midway," Michelle volunteered. All the parents offered to join the girls, but they persisted in reassuring the grown-ups that they were no longer five years old. After agreeing on a meeting point, the two girls skipped off into the land of undiscovered adventures.

At the base of the high-flying wheel, Angela simply stared at the rising cubicles for at least thirty seconds and missed several of her cousin's introductions.

"Angela, this is Troy," she finally heard and then broke out of her daze.

The young teenager was wearing a cowboy hat and had a nice smile. He extended his hand and then pointed to the ride.

"Let's give it a whirl," he said and then whispered, "I been on it four times already today."

"Well, hey, then we should try something new," Angela offered.

"No, it's great."

"But the line is so long."

"It moves fast. Like the ride itself."

It was not the description that Angela wanted to hear, but it left her no wiggle room other than to say she was too scared to go on the Texas Star. She was definitely not going to say that, not in front of her cousin or the two boys. So before long, all four young folks were in the cubicle on a slow climb up the heavens.

Every twenty feet or so, the wheel would stop and gently rock while new folks would be loaded in another cubicle. Finally, after several minutes, the wheel simply rose and fell and rose and fell, just like Angela's stomach. The young girl didn't dare look out the window. Instead, she scrunched as close as she could next to Troy.

Perhaps he misinterpreted her intentions. All she knew was that in the next few seconds, young Troy pulled her head closer. As she neared his face, she did steal a look at her cousin who was in lip-lock with Brad. Rather than pull away, Angela closed her eyes (which she had wanted to do during the entire ride anyway) and meet his lips. She could also feel herself slide even closer into his arms. Here, she would remain until the gondola finally came to its resting place at the bottom of the circle and the operator opened the door.

"Some experience, huh?" the operator said with a wink.

"That was damn fun," Troy gushed.

"First time?" the operator asked Angela as she exited the gondola. At first, she feared that the geezer had somehow detected that she had never kissed a boy in her life—certainly not like that, for at least four titillating, tantalizing minutes. She looked at the operator and came to believe it was basically an innocent question.

"First time on the Texas Star," she clarified with some bravado.

Still in a reverie, Troy remarked, "Jeezus, let's do that again."

"Maybe after a few shows," Angela promised. But in her heart, there was some deep, dark, dangerous desire to see what might happen on that second journey.

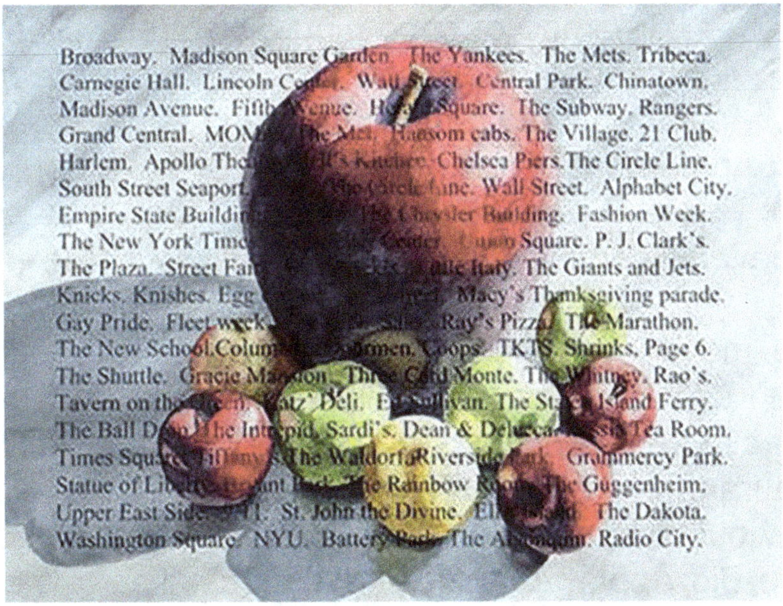

The Big Apple
Watercolor
34 × 27
2009

The Big Apple

Heidi Carlstrom was born in Appleton, Wisconsin, and always thought she belonged in a bigger city.

Part of it was the mall/chill/social life of this Midwestern town. Add to that the lack of any vibrant downtown and the fact that most on-the-ball Appletonians dreamed of moving to metropolitan Milwaukee, liberal Madison, or the big city—Chicago, Illinois.

Truth be told, few locals ever moved beyond the two-hundred-mile radius. According to locals, it was just not done. Consequently, when Heidi announced she was relocating to New York City at the age of twenty-one, it was something of a scandal.

Some whispered that the young woman simply wanted to be away from her parents, who had a violent, bullet-ridden separation five months earlier. Others imagined that she must have been pregnant and felt the need to have an abortion out of state. By contrast, others opined that she was a lesbian and must escape the provincial attitudes in order to find her own life.

None of these hypotheses were true.

Heidi Carlstrom dreamed of becoming an actress. She had played Laurie in her high school production of *Oklahoma* ("People Will Say We're in Love") and enjoyed it more than any experience of her past four years in Appleton. She actually signed a few autographs for the grade-school kids. From that moment, she was hooked on something beyond serving glazed cake crullers at the local Dunkin' Donuts.

When she moved to a studio in Hell's Kitchen, she got her first rude wake-up call. The third floor walk-up studio cost her $2,000 a month. Her acting lesson cost $100 a week. Her job as a waitress at Trellis Restaurant paid about $400 a week. You do the math.

Yes, she would have about three months to achieve fame and fortune in the Big Apple. Against a time clock, it's a difficult ambition to crack. It took her weeks to discover where the agents did business (several more weeks to get her first appointment) and a month to find out where auditions were.

Not surprisingly, Heidi's foray into show business would take more time, more money, and more creativity. Her first solution was to supplement her waitress tips with a part-time job as a tour guide on those double-decker busses throughout Manhattan.

"To your right is Rockefeller Center, where the world-famous Rockettes are trained to kick their heels at least three inches over their heads . . . and we're having a Rockette audition today. You sir, would you like to give it a try?"

"To your left is the Plaza Hotel, built in 1907 . . . where a fictional little girl explores the halls every night. What's her name?"

"Here we are at the Ed Sullivan Theater, where the namesake introduced the Beatles, Topo Gigio, and Señor Wences. He also introduced Elvis to America [pause]. What song did Elvis sing here in 1956?"

Granted, Heidi was given a script, but she added all the involving questions and the audience-participation games to the tour. Her performance netted more tips than any other guide, a higher customer rating than her fellow workers, and earned her the most favored schedule of all employees.

For Heidi, that meant weekend mornings bringing the Big Apple to life for hundreds of Midwestern tourists. On one particular morning two months ago, her tour-bus audience included a theatrical agent who was showcasing his adopted city for his St. Louis cousins, nieces, and nephews. In the course of "the show," he was unable to kick higher than the Rockettes. However, he did enjoy her act.

"Do you have a résumé and head shot?" he asked.

"Martin Hopkins?" Heidi guessed from website photos.

"Yes," the top talent agent in the Big Apple responded.

In the next five months, Heidi has been in a Noxzema commercial, an industrial film for the Cunard Lines, and an "under-five" actor in the soap opera *General Hospital*.

There is more in the works. On the heels of one interested agent, three other agents attended the Saturday bus tour of the Big Apple. Two asked for head shots and résumés. Heidi Carlson has now been cast as a stripteaser in the upcoming movie *Cherry Hill*.

"Oh, what a beautiful morning . . ." the young actress remembers her high school *Oklahoma* experience and sings the signature song to her bus full of tourists. Perhaps there will be an agent on board who is interested in something more than a quasiporno film. If not, Heidi has already gained four more Big Apple tours next week.

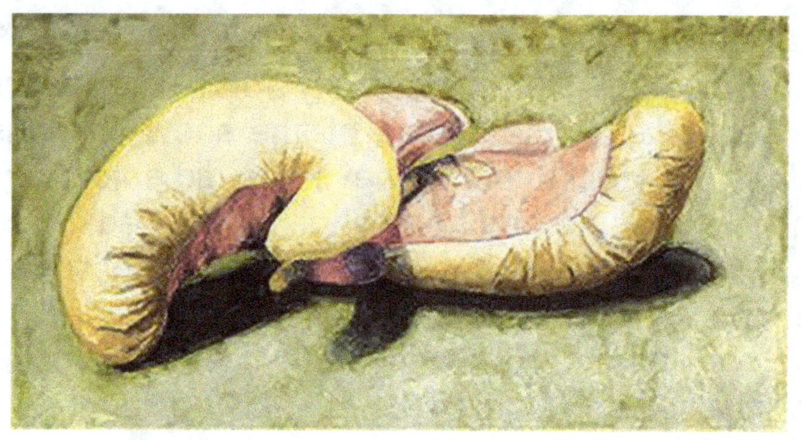

Hanging up the Gloves

At this point, my baby boxing gloves hang from the rearview mirror of my Camaro, in that same goofy position from which other people hang fuzzy dice.

I never quite understood that pink fuzzy dice thing. What's the meaning? On the other hand, I completely understand the dangling boxing gloves. They were a loving gift from my father, Louis "Lightning" Gonzales, when I was born. If you are over fifty, you might remember him. He was briefly the lightweight championship of the world (after defeating Ray "Boom Boom" Mancini). My father's reign only lasted two years, but the ring experience was always with him and, consequently, always with me.

Perhaps that's why I became a boxer in my late teenage years. I was dubbed Junior Gonzales for marketing purposes. Just to whoop up the crowd, I was often introduced as the son of the great lightweight champion Louis "Lightning" Gonzales. After my rather mediocre 7–3 initial record, I began to resent the comparison. When my father died in his early fifties after premature Parkinson's disease and a brain tumor, I absolutely forbade any further comparisons to the legend.

My only silent tribute to him was the set of gloves hanging from my rearview mirror.

Ironically, it is now my only link with world of prizefighting. After my dad died, I had enough money (barely) and enough undamaged brain cells to enroll in Westchester Community College.

It was humbling to be just another kid in the class. Most of these kids had no idea that I was once the center of attention of mano-a-mano gladiator battles. None of them ever knew the ugly, exhilarating thrill of pummeling a foe and raising your winning right arm in victory or the crushing devastation of being knocked out and then needing restorative plastic surgery. On the other hand, I had no idea of the slow drag of poverty or the long climb to self-respect that so many of my classmates represented.

Two years later, I gained an interest in criminal justice. Two years after that, I gained a degree from John Jay College in Manhattan. It's a ticket. For the next thirty years, I will have a job. Given my hardscrabble background, I will undoubtedly have something to offer troubled kids about restarting their lives.

In so many ways, I admire the path I have created for myself.

However, it by no means is a perfect path. Like many others, I have made careless mistakes. One is the unintended pregnancy that will soon come to fruition with my friend Lucinda. Smartly, she does not want to marry me. Of equal importance, she also wants to bring our baby to term, and I will be there to support my isolated son or daughter over the next decades, albeit as an outsider.

As I drive away from our last OB-GYN appointment, I view the red light at the intersection that is just slightly obscured by the hanging baby gloves on my rearview mirror,

I hate to be sexist about this, but if it's a boy, I want him to know the blood that infused his veins. I will place these gloves in his crib and hope that someday, twenty years from now, he will know that his father's side fought for dignity and acceptance in today's world. Maybe he will even hang them from his rearview mirror. Hopefully, he will choose a less pugilistic path to the American dream.

And if it's a girl, basically the same thing, except there will be no boxing gloves in the crib. I just dream that she will fight her bouts in the courtroom as a lawyer. That way, there will never be a need for restorative plastic surgery for a baby as beautiful as my daughter would undoubtedly grow up to be.

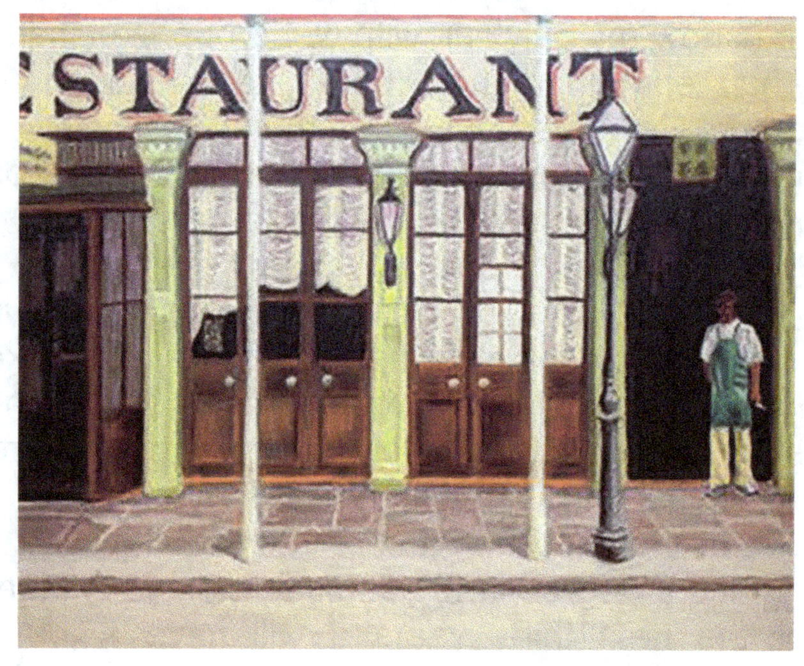

Antoine's
Pastel
34 × 27
2004

Bad Butt Break

As recently as ten years ago, taking a breather from my restaurant prep for a five-minute nicotine hit was not considered a moral weakness—especially here in New Orleans, where hedonism is practically a knee-jerk reaction.

This is, after all, the city where tourists carry go-cups of hurricanes on the streets. It's where middle-aged women show their tits for plastic beads. It's where business leaders hit the strip clubs, vomit at dawn, and sleep away their hangovers until noon. Of course, times change. After Katrina, lots of Habitat for Humanity folks and government engineers descended upon the city. However, it would only take them about twenty-four hours to fall into the "laissez les bon temps rouler" lifestyle of the Big Easy.

Consequently, it always struck me as rudely intemperate when someone would complain about my having a Marlboro Light in the middle of the afternoon.

"Must you intrude on my space by expelling your poisonous smoke in the atmosphere?" a rather large woman scorned me yesterday.

From her accent, I judged her to be from New England. My guess? She was a teacher, probably here on a convention.

I usually let these things go, but for some reason, I just wanted to enjoy my butt without harassment today, so I verbally pushed back. "Yes, I must. Because this is also my space. And it's a large street." I then reached in my front pocket, pulled out a cigarette, and extended it her way. "Would you like one? They are very good. Excellent tobacco."

The woman was aghast. "Are you daft?" she barked at me.

"I'm just trying to be friendly," I said sarcastically.

I could tell this pissed her off. She took my generous offering a few inches from my nose and broke the cigarette in half.

I fought the instinct to erupt. Instead, I took another drag of the Marlboro Light in my right hand. As a courtesy, I rotated ninety degrees and blew smoke away from her. I then stared at the woman who was far too in my face. "You owe me fifty cents."

"You've got to be out of your goddamn mind," she retorted.

"That's what cigarettes cost these days."

"Then that's reason enough to quit. Besides, I just saved you a few days of your life." The woman then reached toward my pocket, presumably to grab my cigarette pack and crush it in front of my eyes. It's not typical of me, but I admit to swatting her hand away.

Who knows exactly how these things get unraveled so quickly? Perhaps it's a verbal version of road rage. One party ups the ante, the next responds with more aggression, and then it just accelerates.

That's when she kicked me.

That's when I said, "Why don't you move your fat ass down the street and find some all-you-can-eat restaurant?"

That's when she said, "Fuck you and your fucking habit." I assumed the F-word was not her usual vernacular. Otherwise, she wouldn't have used it twice in one sentence and paused before each utterance. And then she scurried away.

I thought about chasing her around the corner, but I figured she may have ducked into a Krispy Kreme shop and ordered a half dozen glazed donuts.

It was time to return to the kitchen. I was sure my executive chef was looking at his watch, ready to trade places with me so he could have his afternoon drag of a Newport. However, my butt break had not achieved its mission of punctuating my afternoon and jumpstarting my evening. No, I was not quite ready to return. Instead, I lit a second Marlboro Light and took a satisfying drag. As I looked to my left, I saw a couple walking toward me. Just so I could enjoy my respite in peace, I decided to walk to the other side of the street and blow to my heart's content.

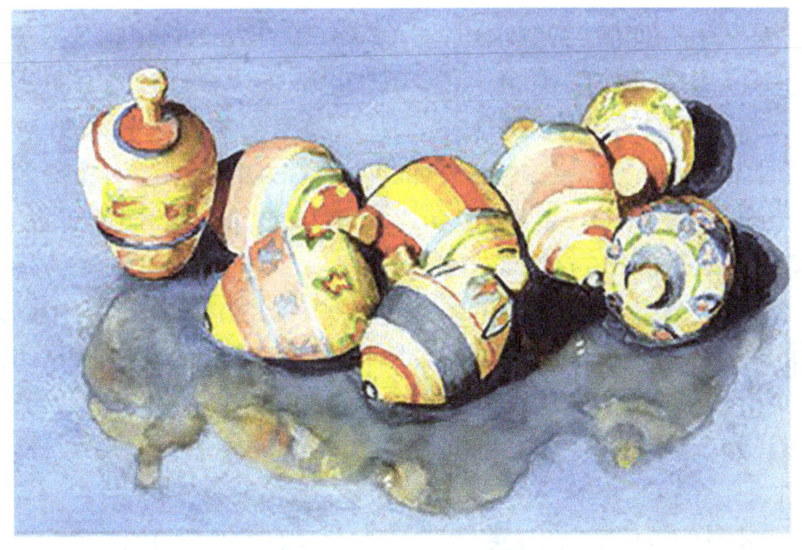

The Spinmeister

There are those ticks, habits, or hobbies that inevitably reveal the inner insecure characteristics of certain characters. For example, Captain Queeg squeezed marbles as if they were weak strawberries to be crushed. John McCain sang "Bomb, Bomb, Iran" in a vain attempt to ameliorate his fun, aggressive stance to our supposed enemies. And then there is Mark Palmer, the widely acknowledged master spinner for every Democratic candidate since the failed presidential election of Ted Kennedy in 1986.

Long ago, he had learned to excuse blatantly stupid responses. When Ted Kennedy stumbled about why he should be elected president, Palmer explained that "it was an ambush, like that unsuccessful one in Iraq by Jimmy Carter." When he was confronted with the Bill Clinton–Jennifer Flowers sex scandal, Palmer excused, "So many women want to 'connect' with this president, and given his stance on women's issues, how can you blame them?" When he was asked to explain Senator Kerry's windsurfer photo, he countered, "He's a man in touch with nature. America celebrates that."

Few of these ploys actually worked. However, the man was considered the best at damage control when a candidate imploded in front of hundreds of thousands of Americans. As a way to ease these tense moments, Palmer would nervously pass the time by spinning wooden tops on a smooth surface while his clients prepared for a press conference or debate.

"How can you stay so calm?" one of Palmer's competitors once asked him before a debate. Mark Palmer then twisted another top and watched it find its balance for several seconds. He then watched it lose its equilibrium and collide into a crash, which amused the spinmeister.

"It's just a matter of time before your guy or mine says something stupid. Once you recognize that it definitely will happen, it makes it easier to handle."

At tonight's debate, it happened in the first fifteen minutes. Palmer's client, Barack Obama, seemed to be asleep at the wheel in front of an aggressive Mitt Romney. For the next seven or eight minutes, it was easily explainable as a lull. However, the trend continued throughout the entire debate.

After about ten minutes, Mark Palmer quit spinning his top and started making notes. "Too many lies." "Frustration with a flip-flopper."

"Inexplicable presidential crises." "No wish to dignify challenger aggression." Then Palmer wrote, "POTUS is just off his game."

Of course, this was the truth. But it was *not* what a spinner is supposed to supply to a horde of news hounds looking for a sound bite.

Palmer had learned to trust his initial instinct. Consequently, "too many lies" became the party line. It did two things: it allowed for a counteroffensive and it explained the president as an honest gentleman.

It convinced no one. The brouhaha of the bad performance gained steam by the hour. After talking with the president, Palmer realized that his last note was in fact the most accurate. POTUS was, in fact, off his game—just a bad night, an evening of bad karma. Everyone's allowed, unless you are running for the head of the free world.

At midnight, Mark Palmer was again spinning his tops alone in his hotel room. How to turn this thing around? How to make most of such a topsy-turvy situation? How to stay upright?

By noon the next morning, Barack Obama was dedicated to the self-deprecating approach. According to Mark Palmer, it offered several advantages: humility, humor, honesty. Until now, none of these traits had ever been the recipe for reelection to the presidency. However, as Palmer repeated and rather nervously spun his top, he opined that it was the best course available.

Six months later, with Obama reelected, Mark Palmer continues to be the spinmeister. In today's world, however, his advice more often than not adheres to the truth rather than the spin.

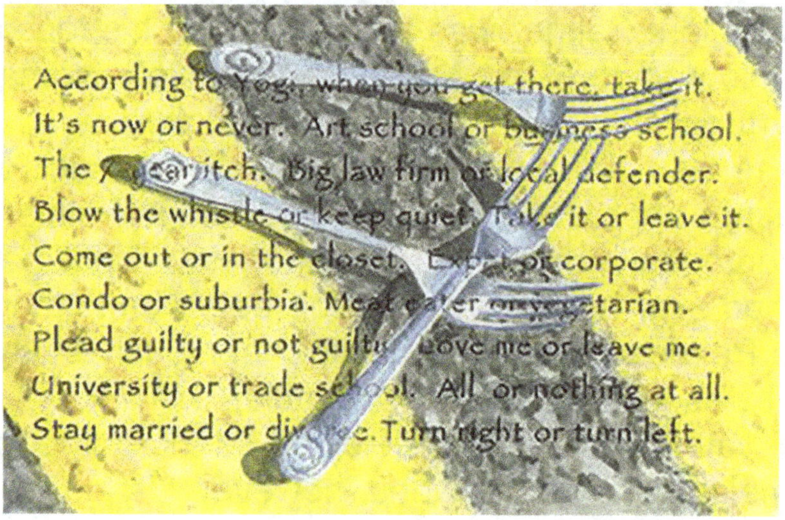

Forks in the Road
Watercolor
21 × 14
2010

Forks in the Road

She had always done everything everyone expected of her. True to her parents' dreams, she had graduated near the top of her class from Columbia Law School and landed an enviable job at a top Wall Street firm. Upon graduation, she had married her college sweetheart in a picture-perfect wedding. Now the two of them lived in a luxury co-op in the Flatiron District of Manhattan with their AKC golden retriever.

However, at the ripe age of thirty-one, Elaine Peterson already felt trapped in some sort of premature midlife crisis. Nothing was drastically wrong. Everything was just so blah.

For the past year and half, she had tried to fight this growing sense of ennui. More exercise at the gym. More weekend getaways with her husband, Michael. More recreation classes. Even more dedication to the law firm. For the most part, the more she packed her days, the more she felt on a nonstop merry-go-round that was eerily joyless.

On the surface, of course, it made no sense. And when all her friends constantly remarked hers was such a charmed, storybook life, it just made matters worse.

"I keep expecting that one of these days you're going to tell us we're becoming grandparents," her mother told her one day.

"Not ready for that," Elaine answered.

"You should make partner at the firm first," her father suggested.

"I don't know that I'm ready for that either," she snapped.

"Oh, sure you are," the parents answered almost in unison. It was the way they always dealt with any hesitation on their daughter's part: stereo encouragement.

Truth be told, that partnership thing was looming. A few of the senior partners had already hinted she was a strong candidate for next year's promotions. This tease did not make her beam. The very prospect of spending the next several decades litigating on behalf of obscenely profitable insurance companies depressed her to no end. It also raised questions. If the job didn't give her satisfaction, why was she pouring so many billable hours into the place? If she didn't really want to be a partner, what the hell was she doing there?

None of these types of questions reared their ugly heads when she took her recreational baking classes. Her hands were busy kneading dough, her mind was focused on timing and temperature, and her artistic side was challenged with decoration. Besides, at the end of every class, there was something tangible to show for her efforts. Usually, it was something gooey and delicious to bring home.

"I like this new hobby of yours," Michael remarked one night, after biting into one of her fruit financiers.

"It may be more than hobby," Elaine answered after a pause.

"What do you mean?"

"I've been thinking about this for the last seven or eight months. I like making these things. I'm good at it."

"They're delicious," he agreed, taking another bite.

"And I'm thinking . . ." Elaine struggled to complete the sentence. "I'm thinking . . . I may want to enroll full time in their professional culinary program."

Her husband stopped nibbling and let this unexpected bombshell sink in. "Wow," he quietly reacted. After a few seconds, he felt he should say something else, but all that came out was another "Wow."

"I want to do this," Elaine asserted. Just saying it aloud was a wonderfully liberating feeling. It was easy. Of course, the curriculum itself would not be. It would take a full year and then several more years apprenticing in a restaurant or bakeshop.

"Have you thought of what you might tell the law firm?"

"That won't be difficult. There are dozens of round-the-clockers who are dying to be partners." She shrugged. "The hard part will be telling my folks that their legal-eagle daughter wants to make brownies for a living."

The very thought of it made her laugh. Then Michael did so, even louder. Then Elaine followed suit, even louder. Even louder. Even louder.

"I haven't seen you so happy in so long," he snuck in between giggles.

"Can't wait," she said. And for the first time in years, she meant it.

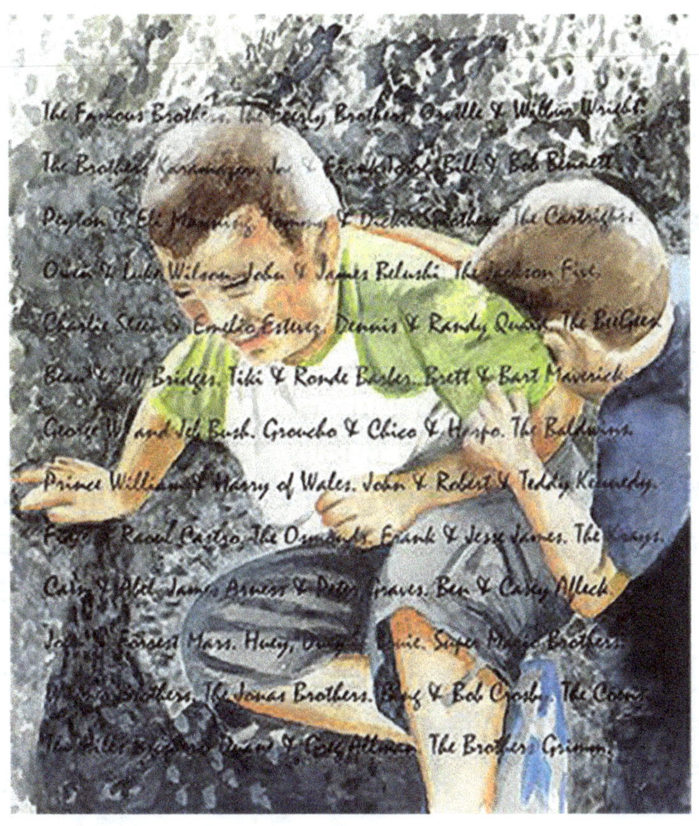

Brothers
Watercolor
28 × 30
2012

Brothers

Everyone says there couldn't be anything worse than having to bury your daughter or your son. I know it was a nightmare for my parents. However, I now speak to you about a less obvious but equally painful loss: my brother, Jesse.

I was only five when my happy-go-lucky older brother was struck by a car, succumbed to a coma, and eventually expired after several days in St. John's Hospital. Because of my young age, I was only allowed to see him for one twenty-minute visit. I am sure that my shock and horror at seeing all kinds of tubes crisscrossing into my silent big brother's body was considered reason enough to shelter me from viewing any further damage.

For three days, I remember waiting at Aunt Margaret's house until my parents would come to pick me at around 10:00 p.m., when the hospital visiting hours ended. "Is Jesse any better?" I'd hopefully ask, and my mom would just cry and run to the bathroom. Left alone, my dad would put his arm around me and say, "C'mon, son, let's go home."

I figured it was bad all by myself. On the fourth night, even my aunt started crying. She walked me out to the curb in the middle of the afternoon and told me that my mom and dad would be picking me up early on that day.

"Is Jesse any better?" I innocently asked.

There was a long pause. Dad finally said, "We'll talk about it when we get home." Once inside the house, they broke the news to me with every understandable cliché that every bereaved parent can possibly muster he will no longer be suffering, he s in a better place, he was at peace, his spirit will always be with us.

All I knew was that I would no longer have my big brother, Jesse, to hug. I would no longer hear his silly giggle. We would no longer watch cartoons together or fight in the driveway or laugh like hyenas afterward.

I think I cried for forty-eight straight hours.

I'm not sure my parents noticed since they were knee-deep in their own grief. I do remember my aunt Margaret asking me to be strong over the next week since my parents definitely "already had all they could handle."

That was thirty years ago, and while I no longer think about big brother Jesse every single day, barely a week goes by that I do not reflect on the loss of brotherhood I endured singlehandedly. In my study, I still have a photo of the two of us hugging in the driveway and laughing our heads off.

Yes, Mom and Dad eventually bounced back (about 50 percent), but they were never the same. They died ten years ago within months of each other, and I remain convinced their early physical degradation was due to the premature grief of burying my older brother.

I wish they could have met my two young sons. My wife and I named the older one Jesse. Since turnabout is fair play, my wife chose the name for son no. 2—Hugh (after her dad).

I watch these two knuckleheads play together, and I feel like jumping over the moon. They are so happy. They are filled with such high jinks. They punch each other. They trip each other. They tickle each other. They fart in front of each. They laugh about it like goofballs.

I love them.

I envy them.

I watch them.

When I do, there are still those days when I want to cry.

The personal computer. The ipod. The microwave.
Anti-lock brakes. The Pill. The DVD. Television.
Cell phones. Luggage with wheels. Air conditioning.
The escalator. Digital photography. The Internet.
The seedless watermelon. Polyester. Antibiotics.
Solar power. Contact lenses. The VCR. Teflon.
Velcro. ATMs. Answering machines. Snowboards.
Plastic. Teleconferencing. The remote control.
Power steering. Egg beaters. Wraps. Blackberries.
Food processors. Hair extensions. Zip-lock bags.
Laser Surgery. Invisible Fence. Digital blackboards.
Icemakers. Google. Home-made, unsliced bread.

The Best Inventions Since . . .
Watercolor
30 × 23
2007

The Best Invention Since . . .

Walter Frederick Morrison had always considered himself a "creative free spirit." In his high school class, he had scored an A in art. He got a B+ in creative writing. More to the point, he was the first-place winner in Junior Achievement. His brainchild? He devised a last-minute printout of Las Vegas odds for every college and pro football game odds. He sold his inside information for $1 at every deli, pharmacy, and fast-food joint in Bridgeport, Connecticut. The net profit in year one: $787. Despite the gambling component, the JA named him the most promising entrepreneur in Southern Connecticut.

It helped the eighteen-year-old gain acceptance at the highly regarded Kelley Business School at the University of Indiana. Here, there were classes in statistics, international business law, and tax accounting. Not surprisingly, these science classes were a washout for Morrison, who resigned from the college rather than flunk out of academia.

Upon his return to Bridgeport, the young man found few want ads in the local newspaper that called for "an amazing entrepreneur." Rather than sit at home, Morrison took a low-paying job as a pastry assistant at the Frisbie Baking Company. Here, his imagination continued to flourish. He dreamed of creating a new pie ingredient based on avocado (no takers). He considered a birthday lattice pie of initials for birthday celebrations (too expensive). He thought of fried pie sections (not enough deep fryers in America).

Discouraged, he took his cigarette break in the parking lot and was struck by a flying pie plate in the forehead. It resulted in six stitches at the local hospital.

The two culprits near his hospital bed promised that they would never again hurl a flying-saucer disk made of Frisbie pie tins.

"You absolutely promise you will never again do this or claim any credit for the idea of ever doing this?" Morrison asked from his hospital bed. As long as he was at it, he asked the attending nurse to come into his room as a witness.

"Never again," the two bakery workers promised. With that, Morrison smiled and slept well that night.

The next morning, he began sketching his new invention and initiated his patent search. The "Morrison slope" is listed on the patent, which was sold to the Wham-O Company—the outfit that also marketed the Hula-Hoop, the Super Ball, and the Water Wiggle. Given America's sudden fascination with UFOs, the Frisbee sold in the millions. You could find them on every beach of the Southeast. On every college campus, students tossed the disk and invented Ultimate Frisbee. Every dog owner bought one to teach their favorite pet the give and take of a relationship.

Ultimately, Walter Frederick Morrison made more than a million dollars
in royalties.

That was fifty years ago. If you ask any inventor, they will tell you that one breakthrough is not enough. According to them, it is part of their DNA. Perhaps that's why Morrison never rested on his laurels. He came up with the idea of putting wheels on luggage but was unfortunately beaten to the punch by an inventor who posted a patent two months earlier. Then he came up with this notion of electronically keeping dogs inside the yard, but the Electronic Fence Company already owned the rights. Yesterday, he was tossing an old Frisbee along the St. Petersburg beach, and when he dug it out of the sand, he found a diamond ring. Suddenly, he thought that perhaps a beach metal detector might be a profitable idea.

Yesterday, the US Patent Office informed him that the patent was issued twenty-four years ago.

"Timing is everything," Morrison admitted to himself. Then he tossed the disk into the sky. It landed on his neighbor's roof. "Wow, I wonder if one could get broadcast signals if one owned a big, huge disk aimed at the heavens." Promptly, he began sketching. If you own DirecTV, you might know the outcome.

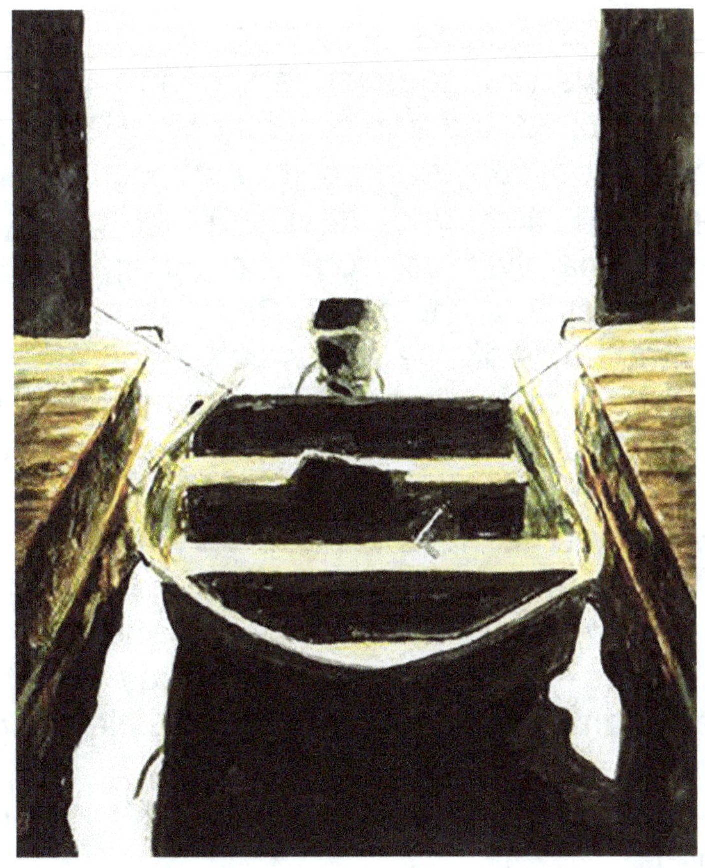

Boat Bag

Andrea Pennington was woefully behind on her upcoming presentation to the Kawasaki Jet Ski Company. It was one of those jump-ball, winner-take-all sales pitches where her company would compete for the lucrative strategic assignment against two other topflight think tanks.

Trouble was, with all the day-to-day assignments from existing clients (several of whom had decided to visit the New York office this week), Andrea was on a 24/7 smile-fest circus and had become entertainer-in-chief for all the muckety-mucks from her Midwest junk-food clients this week.

Now, with four days to go before she would stand in front of these West Coast reputation-making clients, she had nothing. True, her account planners had a quite justifiable, smart strategy. Yes, her creative staff had every suggestion as to how to reach the "new hedonists," as so dubbed and approved by Ms. Pennington.

However, as Andrea had learned through several presentations, the CEO's opening plea and final summation is persuasively clinching or, unfortunately, disastrously crippling. It's rarely a close call. Like political elections, one gets "a feel," then votes, and justifies one's choice on the basis of "the evidence."

Last night, Andrea called her estranged husband in Sagamore, New York, and asked if "the house" was free over this upcoming September 18 weekend.

"Sure, you want me to drive up too so you can meet my new girlfriend?" Richard Pennington kidded her.

"No, I've already met too many of them," she joked back. "I just need a quiet place where I can get away from the nonstop telephones, traffic jams, and the hustle-and-bustle temptations of the city."

"Big pitch?" From their six years together, he knew what such a getaway signified.

"Huge."

"Knock 'em dead," he said. "By the way, I was up a few weeks ago. The leaves have just started to turn, and the lake is stunning. You'll be inspired."

She was. From the moment she smelled the pines outside and walked to the boat pier for old time's sake, she suddenly felt all tension flee from her body.

She and Richard had not quite decided who would end up with this oasis after the divorce. He was closer and would probably use it more frequently. On the other hand, she had the higher power job, and she truly appreciated the restorative quality of the place. She reminded herself not to think about that. No, this was her weekend to dream, make a few notes, and come up with a winning presentation.

The next morning, she brought her handwritten scribbles in a satchel and took out their small, little rowboat/motorboat for a visit to her favorite coffee shop at the next port. This little journey had always worked for her in the past. Here, she would devise the pitch. Despite the fact that the Mercury outboard was only twenty horsepower, it always had plenty of power to negotiate the twenty-minute journey. That is, if it had sufficient gas. Ten minutes from the dock, the engine sputtered.

"Goddamn it, Richard," Andrea screamed to the heavens. "If you're going to bring your blond bimbos out here, at least fill up the tank." And then the sky got dark. Heavy clouds. Wind. Horizontal rain. With no other way back to shore, she began to paddle her way back to the Sagamore house. Struggle. Pause. Paddle. Pray. It ended up taking two and a half hours—Andrea versus nature.

Of course, all her notes were destroyed, which was why she left the soaked satchel in the rowboat. More importantly, the young woman was completely spent. After a twelve-hour sleep, she woke up to crystal-clear skies on Sunday. Aching but confident, she stopped for an eggs Benedict in the village and then got behind the wheel for the five-hour drive back to Manhattan. It felt good to be on the open road and focus her head. Before turning in, she wrote out a few scribbles on three-by-five cards.

"The greatest high, the greatest fear, the greatest thrill is to be one with nature," she began her presentation to the Yamaha Jet Ski marketing staff, who were trained to listen poker-faced but couldn't help smiling at her insight. Without ever referencing her harrowing weekend, she spoke off-the-cuff about confronting the elements. The more she talked, the more the decision makers knew she got it.

Three days later, Andrea Pennington's agency was awarded the Yamaha Jet Ski account. As *Ad Age* reported over the weekend, "Upstart Manhattan outfit upstages West Coast lifestyle groups."

Seven days later, Andrea had a discussion with her estranged husband, Richard, about "the house." Yes, they argued about the gas tank for a few minutes. But then the young woman knew how to leverage the lapse. "It is my good-luck charm," she said and then added, "Given the fact you left me in monsoon, I don't really think you want to negotiate this."

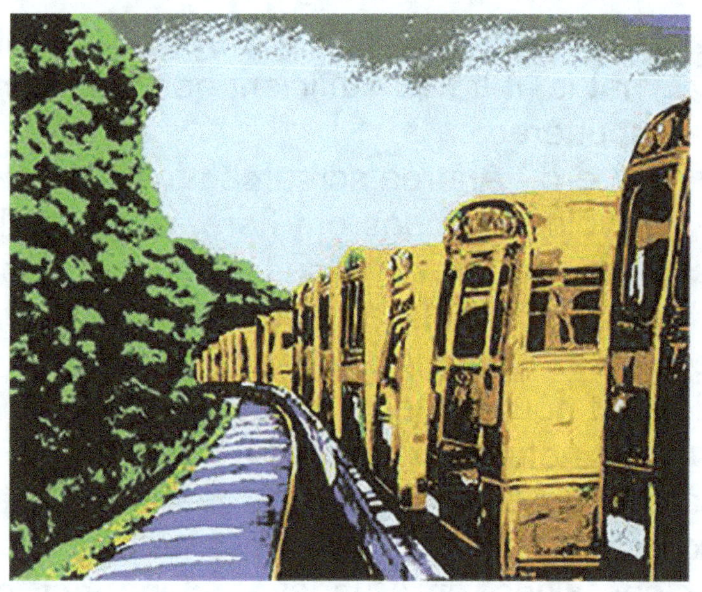

School's Out

Carl Lampe had driven thirty-three kids to and from the Springhurst School for the past forty-one years. On this bright June12 day, it would be the last time he would ever need to back his bus into that tight spot off the Saw Mill River Road. When he pushed that gearshift into park and took the keys out the ignition, he couldn't help but feel his emotions swing between glee and depression.

This gig had never been the career he had envisioned for himself in 1970, after graduating from SUNY–Albany with a degree in history. He had hoped to teach but had unfortunately ignored the advice of his college counselors who repeatedly told him he must switch his major to education in order to do so.

Maybe not, he thought. *Perhaps I could teach at a private school or a Catholic school like St. Matthews . . . or maybe even teach at Springhurst if I promised to get a master's degree in education, if that's so damn necessary.* As it turned out, it was that damn necessary. So as a way to replenish his depleted bank account and save for an advanced degree, he took a related job in the school district—driving the school bus so he could get those young munchkins on the route to learning.

I hate to imply that one practical decision can significantly waylay other dreams, but that's exactly what happened to Carl Lampe. It took him four years to pay off his college loans. By then, he had moved into a modest bungalow, which ate more of his meager salary. One thing led to another, and before the man knew it, he had a decade of school-bus driving under his belt.

Don't misunderstand; he didn't really hate the job. However, that last word—*job*—is the key word here. The 7:00 a.m. trudge in snow, sleet, and rain; the delays from parents holding one finger up until their little darlings were properly dressed; the honking horns from drivers behind him; the occasional flare-ups from the spoiled kids; the emotional belittlement from his neighbors for being just a school-bus driver all made him feel smaller.

However, he did enjoy the two accolades as "Springhurst's favorite school-bus driver," his accident-free driving record and the freedom to pursue his love of history in off-hours and extended summer vacations.

Once finally parked, he sighed. At the time, he was alone, with a few reminders from those whom he had transported over the past nine months. When he reached for the gifts by the gearbox, he reflected on all this. Most of these small white envelopes were marked "Thanks" or "To the bus driver," or "Have a happy summer." On this last day of the school year, many of the parents had given a stipend to the man who safely brought their kids to and from school. Obviously, few knew this would be his last run ever. Alone, in the driver's seat, he opened the envelopes one by one. Ten dollars. Five dollars. A twenty. A ten. Seven dollars (it impressed him that Mrs. Montgomery actually added two dollars to what she could comfortably contribute). A handwritten "*Gracias*" with no money. A gift certificate at Barnes & Noble. And then one which stopped him in his tracks. It was a handwritten note from a child who had sat across him on most of his bus trips. It read, "I liked when you told me about Abe Lincoln. Abby."

On this last day, Carl looked around to see if another bus was ready to park next to him. He hoped not. He did not wish to be disturbed in this moment.

In the distance, he could see two of his co-bus drivers now entering the lot.

The next ten seconds of solitude, reflection, gratitude, and satisfaction can in no way ameliorate forty-one years of hardworking sacrifice. But for the man who truly loved history, it was one of those marking events that until now, he had only studied.

Yes. No. Maybe. I don't know. 1492. Tomorrow.
Montpelier. Midnight. At age 16. Where you left them.
When you're 21. St. Augustine. It's in the mail. Less.
Five kids. Nina, Pinta, Santa Maria. Roses. Pete Best.
Cal Ripken, Jr. Viagra. Gummo Marx. Enola Gay. 1968.
Mexico City. Barry Bonds. Normandy. Three times.
The Jazz Singer. Abner Doubleday. January 1941.
That's where the money is. Mt. Everest. Eight planets.
The number 7. Two blocks on the right. 88 keys. Love.

And the Answer Is . . .
Watercolor
28 × 21
2008

And the Answer Is . . .

Last year, it was estimated that 1,400,000 Americans visited storefront fortune-tellers and tarot-card readers. Call it a fascination with the mystical world beyond organized religion. Call it entertainment. In Angela Murray's case, it was the desire to have someone answer the questions she herself would not.

Will I find the man of my dreams this year? Where will I eventually live? Will I inherit my mother's medical problems? What's the number I should use for lucky lotto?

In some recess of her brain, Angela knew that her wild guesses were probably as good as any of these supposed experts, especially since the five psychics she visited last year gave wildly divergent answers ranging from marriage, San Francisco, colon cancer, number 3, number 862, and "I envision you having a same-sex relationship in the next two months." At $50 a hit, the twenty-seven-year-old woman on a budget was determined to find a more accurate forecaster. However, foolproof predictions had always proven quite elusive.

"Honey, you got a question about what lies ahead for you? I can help figure out your future as well as any damn quack," Angela's diabetic mother told her over a recent dinner. The fifty-year-old divorcee was well aware of her daughter's predilection for third-source prophets. When Angela was a little girl, she adored her talking Cabbage Patch doll, which advised her about the ups and downs of any given day. As a teenager, she turned to the Magic 8 ball, which gave her a plethora of one-word answers like "Yes," "No," and "Try again." Call-in radio Q&A format programs and more serious psychological counseling followed, but the advice was always the same: I can't tell you exactly which path to follow. Only you can answer that question.

However, all these hedges only intensified Angela Murray's search for 100 percent accurate, infallible advice.

Here's a thunderbolt for all you believers in the supernormal! I hate to burst your bubble, but there is no such thing as a 100 percent accurate prediction. Think about it: If there was ever anything close to a sure thing, wouldn't it be used in weather forecasting, at the start of every Wall Street day, and most certainly, before every roll of the dice in Las Vegas? Wouldn't it foresee every plane wreck (and eliminate them)? Wouldn't it calculate which marriages would succeed? Wouldn't it enable us to know our exact moment of death so we could prepare our proper farewells? Why not? Because as most rational people realize, if anything unpredictable can happen, it most certainly will happen.

Such a phenomenon occurred yesterday when Mr. Byron Oliver knocked on Mrs. Murray's door to introduce himself as her new neighbor. Serendipity being what it is, the middle-aged woman followed him to his house for a second cup of coffee and discovered that the man was a collector of board games, including the mysterious Ouija board.

After a few tries, she asked, "How's it work?"

"Involuntary, unconscious movements direct the pointer exactly where the participants wish it would land, so it's a self-fulfilling prophesy."

"Magnificent! May I borrow it for a few nights?" she asked.

"Absolutely," the new neighbor agreed.

That night, Mrs. Murray played the game with her daughter, Angela, who had been in search of answers for decades. "Ask anything," Mom commanded.

"Will I meet the man of my dreams this year?" As soon as she asked it, the pointer seemed to involuntarily guide itself to the *yes* area.

"Wow! And where will I eventually live?" Letter after letter, the pointer seemed to unconsciously stop at *L*, then *A*.

"I knew it," Angela jumped from her seat. "This thing is better than any stupid fortune-teller!" she screamed and high-fived her mother.

This celebration went on for another hour and a half. Every seemingly innocent answer miraculously was the exact outcome Angela wanted. Consequently, her mother had bought Angela a monogrammed, leather-bound set to be enjoyed every evening. Not surprisingly, Angela Murray's next several years unfolded precisely as she imagined they would, could, and should.

PS: On that afternoon of that second coffee between Mrs. Murray and Mr. Oliver, the Ouija question asked was "Might there be a future for us?"

And the answer was . . . (Well, on this one score, I think you may be able to accurately predict it.)

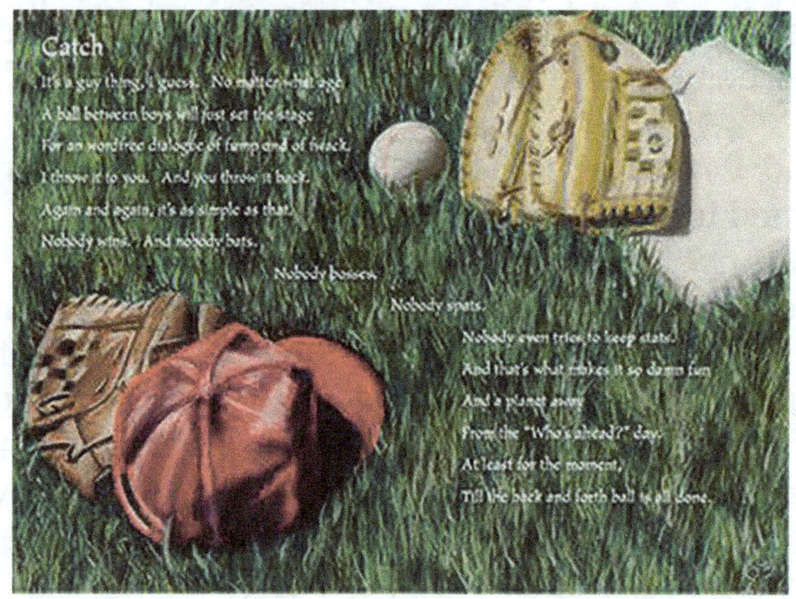

Catch
Pastel
36 × 23
2005

Catch

For years, Rufus Montgomery looked forward to getting to his Cincinnati home by 5:30 p.m. He was rarely late. One reason: Rufus was a bus driver for the Cincinnati Transit Authority, and he fully understood the importance of keeping an accurate, impeccable schedule. His stops included Eighteenth Street at three minutes past every hour, Chestnut Avenue at thirty-one after, and Walnut Street at two minutes before the hour.

An equally compelling reason for his punctuality was his son, Sam, who normally arrived home between five and five fifteen. As a kid, the boy was diagnosed as having ADD (attention deficit disorder), and the assessment surprised neither Mr. nor Mrs. Montgomery. Even as a preschooler, Sam was a bundle of unfocussed energy, running from one end of the backyard to the next. In kindergarten, Sam could focus on building blocks for only three or four minutes, and then his mind would wander off into the distance. By the fifth grade, the school counselor suggested Ritalin and unspecified amphetamines.

As a bullet-wounded escapee from the 1970s drug wars in America, Rufus Montgomery immediately objected to the prescription. "Give me a nondrug route," the dad demanded. "I don't want my son addicted to any damn pill, needle, or medicinal Holy Grail."

Within forty-eight hours, the counselor had a very guarded alternative suggestion. "Change his diet. Cut out all sugar, cookies, and chocolate. Anything that tastes sweet. And keep him active and maybe even exhausted."

Mom changed the lunch box away from Dunkin' Donuts to protein, and Dad bought a baseball.

The following evening, he announced a new regimen. "Sam, every night at 5:30, you and I are going to toss this ball back and forth for an hour. You catch. You throw. I catch. I throw. If you wanna talk, we talk. If you don't want to talk, we don't have to."

"Catch," the kid said and threw the ball to his dad.

"Catch," the dad answered and returned the pitch. This ritual avoided all the pitfalls of ADD: chronic boredom (sitting in the outfield for several innings, waiting for a fly ball), anger management ("We lost, dammit . . . because of me"), and relationship difficulties ("I don't want to bat after him!"). Instead, it was just a steady rhythm of back-and-forth, me and you, fwack-and-fwack, and just enough interest and attention to keep one's mind from leaping into the next yard.

This rite continued for the next seven years, until Sam scored in the top 25 percent of his class and was accepted at Ohio State last September.

It has now been four months since young Sam has been in the Montgomery yard. Perhaps out of habit, Rufus continued to arrive home at 5:30 and pick up his Rawlings glove, only to aimlessly walk around the grass, rather pathetically tossing the baseball in the air and catching it. A few times, Mrs. Montgomery has followed her husband into the backyard and innocently asked if he wanted to throw it back and forth.

"It wouldn't be the same," Rufus mumbled. After thirty years of mumbles, Mrs. Montgomery knew the meaning of his scrambled words.

Last night, the day before Thanksgiving, Sam arrived home, beaming with his newfound freedom as a college freshman, and he flushed with cockeyed optimism. However, somewhat miraculously, the young man somehow remembered the vague roots of his confidence.

"It's 5:30." The kid winked and then tossed the ball to his dad. "Catch?"

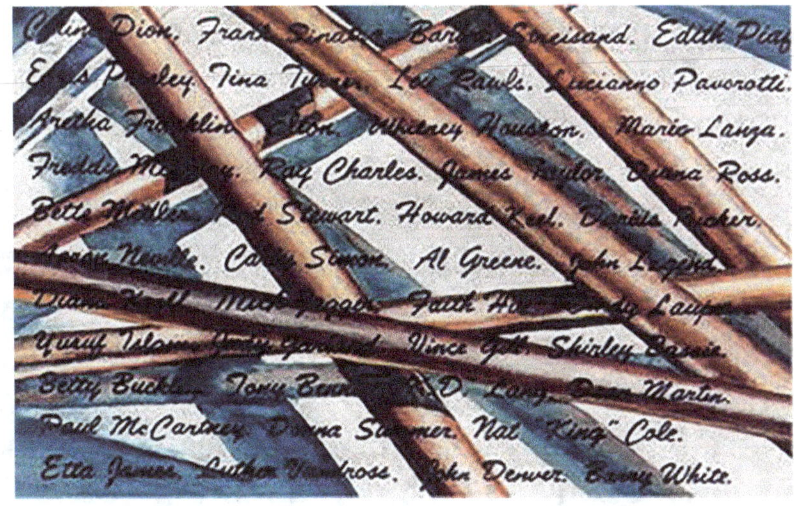

Nice Pipes
Watercolor and pastel
29 × 21
2007

Nice Pipes

Evidently, my grandfather had a sweet singing voice.

In the 1920s, he had come to Missouri as a teenager and was intent on making a musical career on the showboats that plied the Mississippi River from St. Louis to New Orleans. It was the same floating bandstand where Louis Armstrong, Duke Ellington, Bix Beiderbecke, and Jelly Roll Morton played week after week, and it was the pre–American Idol route to musical fame. After all, this was the heyday of jazz, the birth of record players, and a rare, exciting breakthrough for African-Americans in the entertainment business.

My grandfather, a Hungarian-American immigrant named Harry Lang, didn't quite fit the stereotype of the riverboat entertainers. For one thing, he was a white guy. For another thing, all he did was sing. He didn't play the trumpet, sax, piano, or drums. He just made music with his mouth, but from some reviews in the *Memphis Courier,* the *Jackson Journal,* and the *New Orleans Times-Picayune,* that voice was magic.

When I first discovered his almost-forgotten saga, it made me admire him all the more. Here was this color-blind jazz misfit who had chased a dream, had a true affair with show business, and then mysteriously walked away from it all.

In the rearview mirror of history, it becomes somewhat less mysterious. One clue: My dad was born in January of 1928. His sister was born in December of 1929. One month earlier, on October 25, Black Friday changed America
for decades.

Just to put it in historical perspective, anyone with money in the stock market (not my grandpa) lost his or her life's savings. The collateral damage was devastating to everyone. Banks closed. Unemployment rose to 25 percent. A thousand people would apply for the same rare-open job. Thousands of families rode the rails from city to city in search of any odd job. On a more personal family note, the rich patrons who took the riverboats down the Mississippi were suddenly past tense. Some musicians, like Louis Armstrong, relocated to Chicago to eke out a living in the Great Depression. Others with less established reputations had to scramble to make ends meet.

Harry Lang already had two mouths to feed (three with grandma) and chose the latter course. After a full year of itinerant struggle, he became an apprentice steamfitter for the New Deal construction projects that had just begun to appear. Within the next ten years, he had risen to a foreman in the steamfitter's union (since renamed pipefitters). In that time, he and Grandma Lang also had three more kids.

I remember meeting the old man in his seventies. By then, he had built a respectable pipefitting company of twenty-four employees. This lifelong endeavor had provided him, his kids, and his grandkids a hard-earned, good livelihood and a decent future. He owned his home outright in Afton, Missouri. He had visited a few countries outside the United States. He smiled a lot.

However, I never knew he could sing, other than some Christmas carols.

By 1980, my grandfather was into the habit of reminiscences.

Like a lot of old folks who somehow sense that the end is in the crosshairs, he offered me cryptic advice. "Figure out your priorities, my boy. After that, everything just flows—up, down, in, and around— like a beautiful jazz tune."

Four months later, he was dead. At his funeral at the Kutis Chapel in South St. Louis, there were a few people I didn't recognize. For the most part, they were black folks who were in their late seventies but seemed to somehow know my dad.

One, a wizened old man with a gravelly voice, said, "Your grandpa was the best damn singer on the Mississippi. And he paved the way for a lot of folks with good pipes who came after him." The thin octogenarian shook both of my hands and then flashed an amazing, winning smile.

When he walked away, I asked my dad who this stranger was. He looked at the frail figure and then shook his head in admiration of both the attendee and my grandfather's impact on this world.

"That's Louis Armstrong," he said.

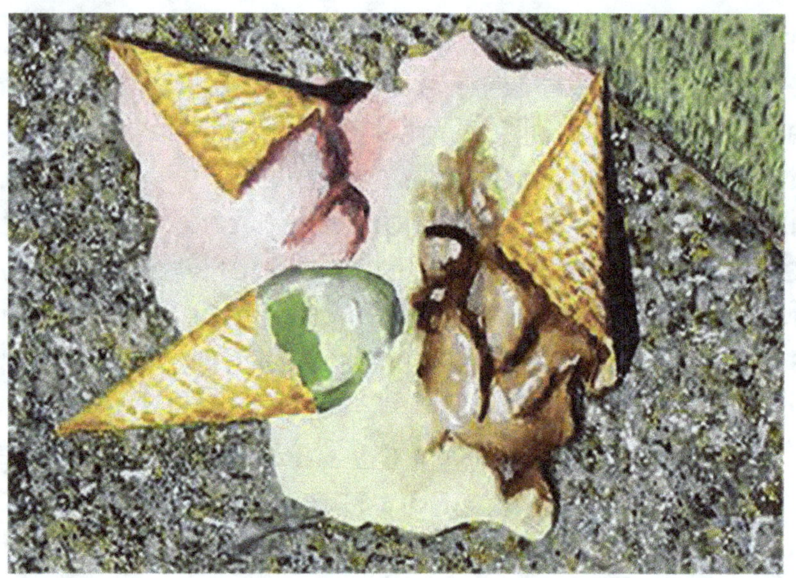

Ice Cream. You scream.
Watercolor
24 × 20
2011

Sweet Nothings

Age fourteen is a spectacular time to fall in love. Just ask Ben van Dusen about the giggles and hugs, the sweet kisses, the whispers, and the coos. For this young man, it was all so new. And it was all so wonderful.

However, as Ben would soon learn, it was not such a great time to fall in love twice, with two different young women.

It started innocently enough with a spring romance in the local high school. The young woman, Abby D'Angelis, was considered the absolute hottest freshman at Dobbs Ferry High School. In addition, she was smart and nice and open to Ben's awkward advances. For months, they walked hand in hand in town and smiled a lot.

However, there was a built-in time-out on the horizon: Ben's upcoming summer trip to Spain. It was officially dubbed a community service camp, but as every privileged kid knows, there would be fun. In Malaga, he met twenty-four like-minded kids who were interested in an escape from their local surroundings.

Ginger Salazar, from New York City, was one of those kids.

"Do you have a girlfriend in Dobbs Ferry?" she asked young Ben while walking along the beach.

"No one like you," he answered, dodging the details of his life in Dobbs. Ginger then squeezed his hand even tighter, and he squeezed back.

Over the next three weeks, things progressed (as the kids say). And when there was a respite, Ben was able to text Abby about how much he sorely missed her.

"Me too," she texted back. "If you want, I will come with your parents and meet you at the airport."

"Whoa! Not a good idea," Ben texted back. "I really should spend those moments to thank my parents for this growth opportunity. It's only fair." As he hit the last word of that sentence, he was surprised at just how good he had become at compartmentalizing his affections.

Within twenty-four hours after landing at JFK, Ben reconnected with Abby and was amazed at how much he missed her sweet smile and the envy of every other young guy in town. By the same token, he had spoken with Ginger every day since returning and missed the exotic times they both shared.

To his dismay, it would all collide tonight at Riverfront Park, where he had agreed to share a blanket for the concert with Abby. Having earlier told Ginger about these events, she invited herself by noon to share her blanket with Ben.

"Oh, no," Ben protested. I'd rather meet you in Manhattan. Much more exciting."

"I'm already on the train," Ginger reassured him.

Consequently, after much Sturm und Drang, Ben van Dusen decided to try his amateurish best to burn both ends of the candle. He spent the first thirty minutes with Abby, then excused himself for a bathroom break at the train station, where he met Ginger and camped out with her for about twenty minutes, and then volunteered to buy her an ice cream cone.

"Strawberry," the young New Yorker suggested. "Don't be long."

As he walked toward the ice-cream truck, he visited Abby, who asked with some pique, "Where were you?"

"Waiting in line at the ice-cream truck. But I didn't know what flavor you wanted."

"Pistachio, stupid. You know that," Abby answered. "And don't be too long."

After buying himself a chocolate cone, Ben van Dusen bought ice creams for his two young women in waiting. Somehow, the forethought of how to deal with the extra cone never quite occurred to the boy. In a slight stroke of luck, he bumped into beautiful Heidi Vail of Irvington. In this collision, all three cones dropped on the asphalt and quickly melted as the creams mixed with one another. He immediately bent down to retrieve the mess, but he knew that the five-second rule did not apply.

"My fault, "Heidi said. "C'mon, I'll replace them."

Ben was tempted, but he had the sudden good sense to pass on this particular invitation. Somehow, he instinctively knew that two young women were more than enough to handle, especially at his age.

Feeling exhausted by the charade and somewhat cowardly, he climbed the steep hill and walked toward his parents' home in the village of Dobbs Ferry. Along the way, he texted Abby and Ginger the same message. "Sorry, I don't feel well. Don't want to get sick around you." Within two days, he would break up with both of these women due to personal conflict as the football season neared.

Age fifteen is a spectacular time to fall in love. Just ask Ben van Dusen who now has a single-minded fling and often whispers sweet nothings to a young woman called Heidi Vail.

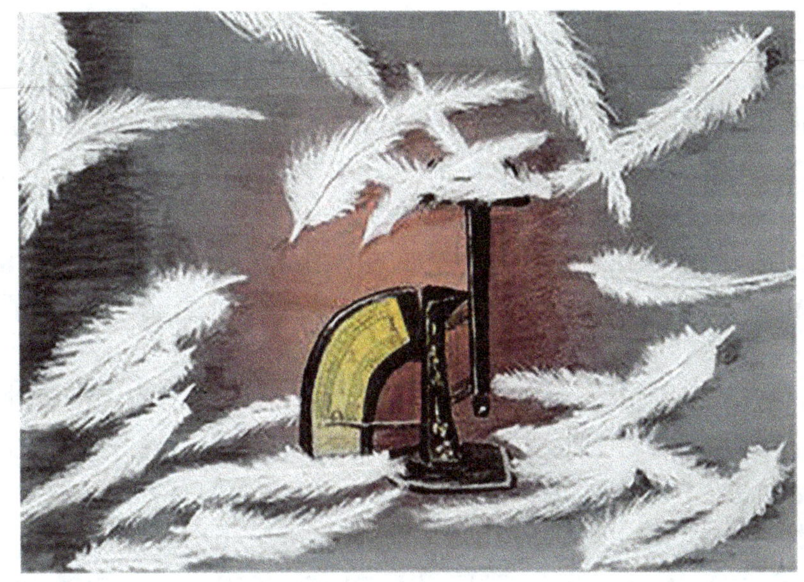

Featherweight
Watercolor
28 × 21
2013

Featherweight

From the age of sixteen, Luis "Little Lightning" Menendez was considered one of the brightest prospects in the Golden Gloves championships. Part of it was the kid's ease in making the 130-pound featherweight class. While other young boxers had to dehydrate themselves in steam rooms for hours (and consequently weaken themselves), Luis simply avoided liquids for the day and normally came in a pound or two under the weight limit.

However, his leverage in the ring extended well beyond mere weight. At 5'9", he was a lanky boy in his class with superb reach of 71". Given the fact that he trained at least four hours a day, he had absolutely no fat on his frame. But his biggest advantage was that incredible hand speed, earning him the nickname Little Lightning. The punches could come in a barrage of fifteen to twenty hits in the space of ten seconds. True, his sudden salvos rarely resulted in a knockout since they were body blows, but the effect was the same. His opponent would typically sag and then stagger, at which point, the referee normally waves his hands and holds up Luis's gloved arm in victory.

Seven years ago, that was the exact routine in Luis's national Golden Gloves victory over a worthy East St. Louis combatant named Emil Washington. The fight was stopped at 1:53 in the first round after Luis bombarded his opponent with a blitzkrieg of explosive punches.

At this point, it would be nice to point to a happy ending for Luis and his family. Unfortunately, real life doesn't always script itself so neatly.

At his parents' urging, the kid signed a contract with the well-known boxing promoter, Max Bender. For the struggling South Carolinian family, the bonus meant paying off the parents' mortgage and guaranteed three professional bouts for Little Lighting. After one initial victory, he was surprisingly outpointed in his second bout ("Foul," fans protested. "Bullshit," Max screamed). However, the knockout Louis suffered in his third bout began to shake everyone's confidence.

Luis assuaged his bruised ego the way many losing boxers do—with food.

By the time of his next bout, he could not meet the 130-pound professional limit for featherweights, and that fight had to be cancelled. Unfortunately, he also missed the 135-pound weight limit for his scheduled-and-then-cancelled lightweight bout. Not surprisingly, he easily met the 147-pound limit for his July welterweight bout but was easily knocked out within one minute of the first round. The same thing happened in the next fight and the next. And the next thing you know, Max Bender gives up on the boy.

For the next two years, the grade-school graduate once known as Little Lightning filled takeout orders at the local Sparta, South Carolina, Burger King every afternoon. The kid also did four hours of sweat-heavy roadwork every morning. Swallowing his pride as the one kid who escaped the slums, he found the courage to beg his Golden Gloves coach, a man named Bobby Gold, to retrain him as a featherweight. More roadwork, more sweat, unfortunately, balanced by more years on his growing frame.

You wouldn't think twenty-four is old in any sport. However, with a losing record in the boxing ring, it's Methuselah.

Partly driven by his own once-in-lifetime experience with the champion, Bobby Gold, Luis's Golden Gloves trainer, was relentless in this pursuit.

"You're only future is as a featherweight," the trainer told Luis and reminded him of this mission every single day by throwing feathers over the weight scale. Inspired by the tableaux, the kid dropped eight pounds, then three more, then two more, then no more.

At four pounds over the limit, one can hardly be called featherweight.

However, Luis Menendez instinctively knew that was his only chance to escape the takeout window at Burger King.

As he had pitifully observed in his earlier Golden Gloves days, he recreated the regimen of the overweight/out-of-class boxers. After initially failing the weigh-in, he went into the sauna, took diuretics, did three nonstop hours of aerobics, and weighed in the nude. He met the 130-pound requirement by 1.2 ounces.

"You are officially a featherweight," the obese official announced. "The fight is on!"

Proudly, Luis Menendez hugged his promoter. Sadly, the kid somehow had a very bad hunch that the toll of meeting the weight would show its effects a few hours later. It's awful to go into a bout with a bad hunch. But it's better than never ever going into the ring again and bagging whoppers for the rest of your life.

"Ladies and Gentlemen, two excellent featherweights . . ." the announcer whipped up the crowd.

The gaunt man once called Little Lightning took a deep breath, put on his robe, rehearsed his once-famous nonstop jabs, and danced through the crowd of the sparsely-filled auditorium.

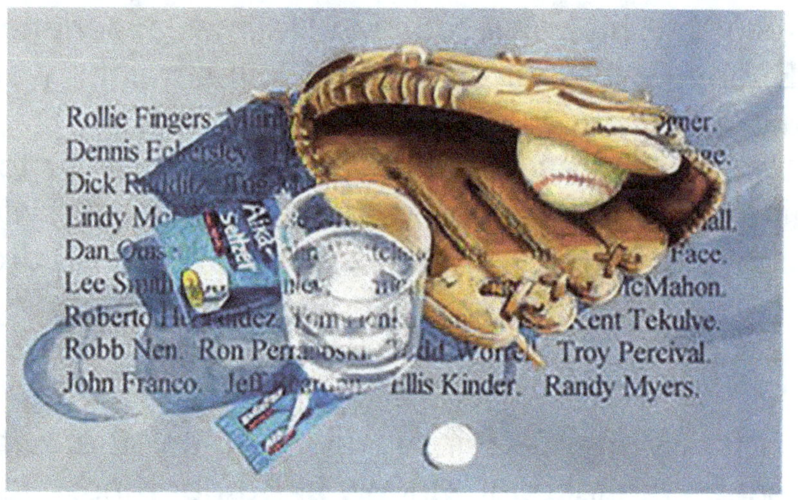

Great Relievers
Pastel
24 × 20
2010

The Great Reliever

When Tony LaRussa walked to the mound in the eighth inning and touched his left arm, everyone at Busch Stadium breathed a sigh of relief that Hooter Haskowitz would soon be trotting in from the bull pen for his umpteenth save of the season.

As with most major leaguers these days, he has his own theme song that rallies the fans. His is an unusual but apt choice: the familiar commercial jingle of Alka-Seltzer (for which he earns $87.23 royalty every time the music accompanies him to the mound). All the fans know the ditty. The organist plays a small lead-in, and then the crowd sways and sings, "Plop, plop, fizz, fizz. Oh, what a relief it is. Plop, plop. Fizz, fizz," etc.

The liaison with this drug company has ironically been a boon for thirty-eight-year-old Haskowitz. He is often called the Oh-what-a-relief-he-is guy or the Fizz, Fizz Wizard. If you follow baseball, you know that the future Hall of Famer's reputation isn't all a marketing miracle. For those of you who love statistics, here are a few: a career 2.86 ERA and an impressive three strikeouts to walk ratio. Want more? Four hundred sixty-seven saves.

On the mound, Hooter is an impressive impresario. As he takes the rosin bag and violently throws it into the grass, the St. Louis fans know that their favorite reliever is in the zone. His first pitch is a 96 mph strike that surprises Chipper Jones of the Atlanta Braves. The crowd roars. Hooter picks up the rosin bag and throws it to ground with even more venom.

As the thirty-eight-year-old looks into the night sky to what he instinctively knows is one of his last few major league years, he can't help but flash on his serendipitous journey.

Like most late-inning firemen in the majors, he started as a high school ace. If you ever saw the kid's repertoire, it was impossible not to think he would end up in the majors. Even as a sophomore, the lanky six-footer had a 90 plus mph fastball, a wicked curve, and a sneaky change that made batters look like T-ball spastics. But perhaps his most astonishing trait was the confidence with which he challenged each batter. As he told a local reporter from the *Terre Haute Examiner*, "I don't care if the bases are loaded and the guy has a 3–0 count, I believe he's going down. And so's the next batter. And so's the next."

That was the kind of quote that attracted the St. Louis Cardinal front office. With a glowing report from the scouting system, young Charles "Hooter" Haskowitz raced through the minors and was the pitching star of the AAA Memphis Redbirds within a year.

As they say in baseball, the kid was ready.

The big-league step became automatic when the Cardinal's ace reliever, Mickey Brennan, was charged with a DUI accident that injured a twelve-year-old female. Public sentiment immediately turned against the reckless closer. Always careful about their public image, the St. Louis club sat by quietly while Brennan was convicted of manslaughter. It was the end of the Irishman and the beginning of the young Indianan.

The kid, when twenty-one and the anointed closer of the St. Louis Cardinals, promised himself he would never fall into the same trap that the heavy-drinking Brennan had. Like most young men, he liked his alcohol. Unlike most, he tended to pace himself with occasional Alka-Seltzers along the way, and he had a personal vow that he would never get behind the wheel after a night on the town.

When asked in his midtwenties his secret to success, he joked, "Like Alka-Seltzer, you've got to save the day and deliver any night and on every big occasion."

It became a commercial. It became his theme song. It became an innocent, inextricable legend that benefitted both parties.

Forget it, Hooter Haskowitz now told himself. *Concentrate on the sucker who is standing at the plate.*

On the mound in these sunset years, Haskowitz hurled the rosin bag into the turf and stole a glance at the adoring standing crowd. The great reliever then glared at the batter and unleashed a nasty curve.

Chipper Jones took a desperation swing at a sinker and missed by at least three inches—the last out, another high. As usual, the fans in red went nuts. Even without the organist, they chanted, "Plop, plop, fizz. Fizz. Oh, what a relief it is." Another $87.23. Another night. Another amazing save.

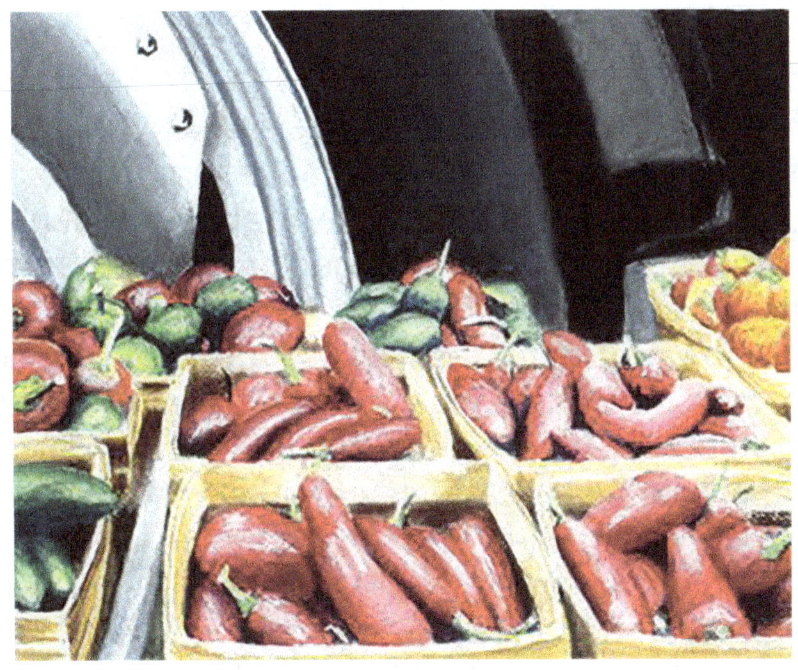

Tractor Peppers
Pastel
26 × 22
2013

Two Lonely Locavores

"Ed, what did you pull from the earth in the past twenty-four hours?" Yvonne Martinez asked as she had done every Friday morning when she viewed the array of glistening produce in the Taos town square.

Ed Curry answered autocmically. "They're all fresher than anything you'll ever find in the A&P," he said and then walked past the peaches, the corn, and the brussel sprouts toward his tractor display, which always showcased his daily special. He then looked down with pride at his last-loaded baskets. "I plucked these Anaheim chilies at five in the morning. Unless you plant 'em in your own backyard, you ain't gonna find anything fresher."

She picked one up and felt the firmness of the bright-red flesh. "Aren't the Aneheims usually green?"

"When they're picked early and shipped to the grocery chains, but these are at peak and packed with more vitamin C."

"Salsa?"

"You can do better than that," he teased.

"Chile rellenos?"

"Interesting."

"A roasted red pepper soup?"

"Bingo! I think your customers would love that at this time of year. And I've got some fresh cilantro." He grabbed a bunch and then opened up an accordion file. He paged through his notes until he found the one sheet he wanted.

"Yvonne, I know you don't really need a recipe, but here's how I make it." He then handed her the pretyped paper. "A little dollap of sour cream can cut the heat."

"I prefer a thin toasted slice of chèvre," she answered with a smile.

"That's why you're the chef," the farmer answered and handed her two pounds of ripe Anaheims.

The two locavores had enjoyed their joint interest in the freshest locally grown fruits and vegetables for three years, albeit from slightly perspectives.

Ed Curry came from a family of farmers a few miles outside of Taos. As a young boy, he loved the land but never liked the isolation. When he discovered the green grocery business in his late twenties, it was a godsend, especially since he linked it with homegrown recipes, which made him something of a local celebrity, at least in the local newspapers.

By contrast, Yvonne Martinez was the Mexican-born chef and proprietor of La Fresca Locale. Two years ago, she began featuring produce from the neighborhood farmers. Not surprisingly, the young divorcee's favorite provider was Mr. Curry, at least partly because he enjoyed cuisine, particularly hers.

In the small town of Taos, rumors of course swirled. Most locals assumed that their relationship must include wild X-rated sex. They didn't really know Ed or Yvonne. Despite their passion for food, both were incredibly shy when the subject veered away from recipes or organic gardening. However, there was an undeniable spark there, and it was fed by the fact that both had agreed to collaborate on a cookbook tentatively titled *Locavore Viva!*

As part of that process, Ed had taken up the practice of stopping by her popular cantina on Saturday nights after an afternoon on the farm. Ostensibly, the purpose of his visit was to enjoy her latest creation and compare notes on recipes. On this particular Saturday night, he brought a gift.

"Do you have some good balsamic?" he asked as he entered the door, carrying a brown paper bag. "I picked these strawberries this afternoon, and they are exploding with flavor, especially with a little drizzle. Some of your favorites might have an orgasm." Yvonne took the bag and gave him a safe kiss on the cheek.

When the tables had emptied and she had waved good-bye to her waitstaff, Yvonne brought out the marinated strawberries. Under candlelight, the two compared notes on the red pepper soup and improvised a new recipe for a Pico de Gallo salsa. Between the notes, they both enjoyed the strawberries, the liquid of which not-so-innocently dripped from each of their lips. Both noticed. Both turned their heads away like junior high school students.

"When's our deadline for this cookbook?" Yvonne asked, cleaning her chin with a napkin.

"Ten weeks. Late autumn," Ed answered, accustomed to thinking in seasons.

After a pause in the candlelight, she looked out the window onto the dark, deserted street. In this town of five thousand locals, it had the same silence every Saturday night. Sure, the population swelled during ski season, but the town shrunk during the year. Most were decent people. The man across the table was more than decent. In fact, all of a sudden, it sruck her that he was amazingly simpatico.

"I will miss this collaboration," she admitted and then looked him in the eye.

Momentarily embarassed, he gathered steam and then reached for the plumpest, drippiest strawberry in the bowl and carefully placed it between her lips. It was the sexiest move she had ever enjoyed—at least for ten weeks, until autumn, when a very different physical collaboration came to fruition.

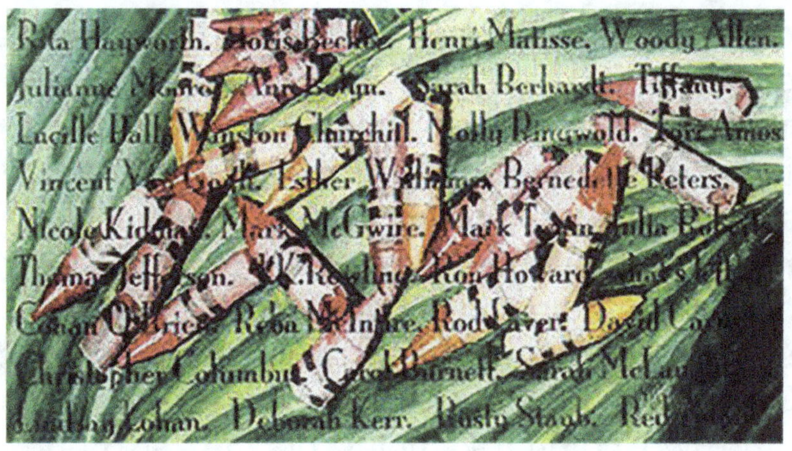

Redheads
Watercolor
24 × 17
2005

The Redheads

My mother named me Ginger because, when I was born, I had bright-red hair, and there were already four girls named Jennifer in the nursery. As a young girl, I never much loved the name, but I supposed it was better than Blaze or Begonia or Robin.

It's a funny thing about names. I suppose you grow into them. I had a grade school friend, Camera, who loved to take photos. I knew a kid named Snow who was a pretty-darn good skier. I, however, never learned to bake gingersnaps. I simply accepted the name as an easy-to-remember handle for a fragrant, tasty, redheaded young woman.

In my teens, when most of my girlfriends began adding blond highlights to their hair (or turning it 100 percent platinum), I somehow resisted the trend and solidified my moniker as Ginger. I liked the fact that most people thought it immediately stereotyped me as a natural woman (after all, who would intentionally tint their hair the color of a root vegetable?).

"Are those freckles forever?" a four-year-old pointed to my face and asked me on my first day teaching preschool.

"I think so," I responded with a smile.

"You think mine will ever go away?" the young redhead innocently asked.

"Sometimes they do, but sometimes you get real lucky and those 'angel kisses' stay on your face for as long as you live." It was the same advice my mother had given me twenty-two years ago when she named me Ginger instead of Jennifer.

"Will those freckles go away?" a young boy asked his teacher on his first day of preschool.

Blake "Rusty" Barker had become accustomed to the question. For the past six years, he had taught at the Montessori and knew that his flaming-red hair would automatically be a curiosity for every new student. As he had learned to accept, it was not the stereotypical detriment that others endured. For example, African-Americans actually suffered discrimination, Latino-Americans were often accused of being illegal, and Asian-Americans were automatically expected to be smart in math even if their true bent was art.

Just to cement the point, Rusty Barker always began his first day of class with a freestyle painting using Crayola crayons.

"I want you to make two drawings," he said. "The first one is the way others see you. The second one is the way you see yourself."

I met Blake at our first lunch in the teacher's lounge when he was looking at the hand-colored masterpieces of his first-day students.

"Wow, that is one fiery-red explosion," I said as I viewed the impressionistic creation. He looked up and smiled. I extended my hand as a means of introduction. "My name is Ginger, and as a real redhead, I am going to guess that your student is coming to grips with being the only different color in a class around her."

"She seems a little feisty," he answered.

"She feels unusual."

"She shouldn't."

"It's just another word for special," I responded, sounding like my mother.

The man looked back at the abstract burst of various shades of red. He then raised his head as if he recognized something simpatico.

"Welcome to Springhurst," he said as he eyed me up and down.

He then invited me to sit next to him. I simply smiled, believing that I may have made my first on-the-job connection.

"My name is Rusty," Blake empathetically announced for the first time in his life.

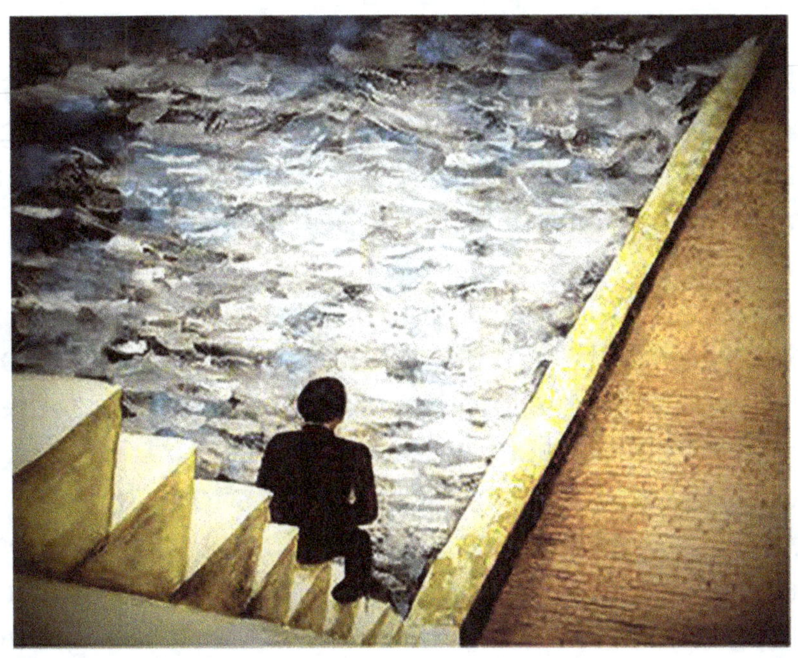

A Penny for His Thoughts

This was now the third straight morning that Dominik Voytka had peered into the deep Vltava River, looking for answers. So far, those cold lapping waters had offered none. However, by today, the man needed a decision.

For the past two months, he had weighed the advantages and disadvantages of immigrating to the USA. If you are an American citizen reading this story, you might well ask, "If you can, why not?" Such is the ethnocentrisms of even the most jaded American.

Dominik Voytka, however, was a torn man. On the one hand, he had a PhD in philosophy from the Charles University in Prague, had been recently honored with the highly coveted Aquinas Award, and was being actively courted by topflight American universities like USC and Columbia. It was undoubtedly a glide path toward intellectual and, perhaps, even social acceptance in a new country.

On the other hand, he had roots in the Czech Republic. He had a lovely wife named Sophia, who both admired and encouraged his dreams. In his late teens, he had supported Václav Havel's rise to power, and that had brought out a potent patriotic sense of independence in him. On a more personal level, he had eighteen first cousins within a thirty-mile radius of Prague, and all of them lionized him as the most successful person to ever bear the Voytka surname.

To his surprise, Dominik's parents actually, albeit reluctantly, supported the move. It had taken the professor several weeks to share his dilemma with his mother and father. Both were extremely proud of their only child's achievements.

Both looked forward to many Christmases together. However, both had lived through hard times under Soviet domination and had always hoped for a better life. Most germane to this quandary, both had promised themselves (and their son) that their greatest goal in life was to encourage absolute, unfettered freedom to dream for him, if that were ever possible.

Who is to say that's possible in the United States? Dominik asked himself.

Like most Europeans, he was puzzled by America's embrace of military escalation and street-level gun violence, the growing gap between the haves and have-nots, and a morally reprehensible intolerance to minorities.

As he tossed a coin from hand to hand in anticipation of a decision, he looked into the river. How could he not just make a damn decision and live with it? Before doing so, he fell back into the trap and considered what he already had.

He already lived in an imperfect country. The economy was dependent on the damn Euro (which was completely beyond his control). However, the social services were good. The history of Czech achievement was impressive: Sigmund Freud, Antonin Dvořák, Franz Kafka, Josef Sudek, et al. Perhaps even more seductive, the people in this country somehow believed that their best days were absolutely ahead of them. He compared that with a feeling he had after speaking with his American friends.

Close call, the intellectual mumbled. He then looked at the coin in his hand and recognized it as an American penny. Almost instinctively, he started flipping it up from his right hand to his left.

Not surprisingly, in a predictable fifty-fifty ratio, it landed heads, then tails, then tails, then heads, etc.

Closing his eyes for a second, he considered outcomes. Then he perked up wide-eyed with a satisfied smile. He gazed into the deep philosophical waters of the Vltava River. He tossed the penny in the air. It seemed to travel in slow motion as it reached his left hand. His fingers closed around the coin.

Dominik Voytka instinctively knew the answer.

Without even looking at the coin in his closed left fist, he hurled the penny into the river and walked across the Charles River to his home in Prague. He hugged his wife Sophia and created his lesson plan for the university classes that he would face in the coming week and for many weeks to come.

PS: Two years later, he won the Nobel Prize for his philosophical treatise called "The Role of Emotion in the Scientific Study of Philosophy." All of Prague celebrated.

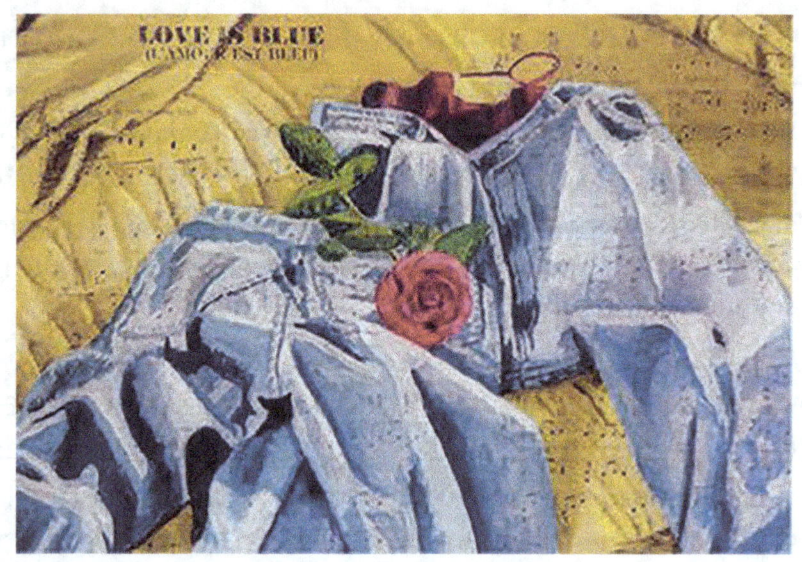

Love Is Blue
Watercolor
30 × 24
2003

Love Is Blue

If Tanya Kellogg had known she would end up meeting someone so warm and wonderful, she may have never accepted the job two thousand miles from Dallas. At least, that's what she had begun to think after her last few mornings with Andy Blake.

They had met in the Food Emporium a month ago, when their carts collided in the produce aisle. She was hurriedly shopping for that big dinner when she would announce this new position to her parents. "Sorry" was all she said at the time as she untangled her cart from his. Looking down at her overflowing basket, he smiled back at her and asked, "Big party?" This led to some welcomed recipe from him on how to grill portobello mushrooms. That led to exchanging phone numbers. Within twenty-four hours, they were in bed together.

It was an atypical spontaneous act for Tanya Kellogg. After her MBA from Northwestern, she had moved back to Dallas, where she continued to do her homework and rise through the ranks to assistant marketing director of Neiman-Marcus. It didn't leave all that much time for love. Yes, she had a few multimonth romances, but her status as a highly paid, successful young woman had proven problematic to most men her age.

Andy Blake was not those other guys. As the sous-chef at the Mansion on Turtle Creek, he exhibited no gender-competitive hang-ups.

In so many ways, he was the perfect mate. Yes, he had taste. But he also lived in the minute and had a wicked sense of humor—an itch that no other woman had scratched in him. Besides, he could make a mean breakfast, which he had done every morning in her apartment for the past week.

Why now? Tanya mused to herself as she stumbled out of bed, attracted to the wafting smell of French toast. At first, she rationalized these last-minute second thoughts to the fact that she had already given notice at Neiman-Marcus and felt a workless freedom she had never before enjoyed. Perhaps it was also because both knew their days together in Dallas were numbered. Maybe this whole thing was a holiday fling. When he presented a freshly picked red rose and said she looked absolutely stunning in her rumpled bathrobe, Tanya couldn't help but think it was something more.

She had been thinking of bringing up the subject ever since she had boxed many of her belongings and FedExed them to California. After all, in the fifties and sixties, lovers did this all the time. Granted, it was usually the man who got a new job in some new city, and the woman automatically followed. But hey, times change. Don't they?

She took a sip of her freshly squeezed orange juice and asked as nonchalantly as she could, "Why don't you join me on the West Coast?"

Andy chuckled and then responded, "Because, honey, I've got a job that I love and a place that needs me."

"I need you," she soberly answered.

He reached across the table and gently brushed her cheek. "Don't think I haven't thought about it."

They jabbered about the nonstop communiqués they could have with e-mail, Facebook, Skype, and telephone. Then she dressed. Then after the longest, most tender good-bye hug, she took the cab to the DFW airport.

It was the job she had always dreamed of landing. On Monday, she would be announced as the chief marketing officer for Levi Strauss in one of the greatest cities of the world—San Francisco. In this economy, dozens of qualified people had begged for the plum position, and she had been the chosen one. However, she was crying.

Twenty minutes later, her cell phone rang.

"See, I told you we'd stay close," Andy said. "I just booked a ticket to come see you three weeks from now. I already miss you. Madly."

Tanya eased back in her seat and gushed all the love words that she had always been so reluctant to release her whole life. As Andy listened, he thought perhaps he should run off a few résumés for his upcoming visit. After all, there were more than a few four-star restaurants with needs of an accomplished up-and-coming chef in the Bay Area.

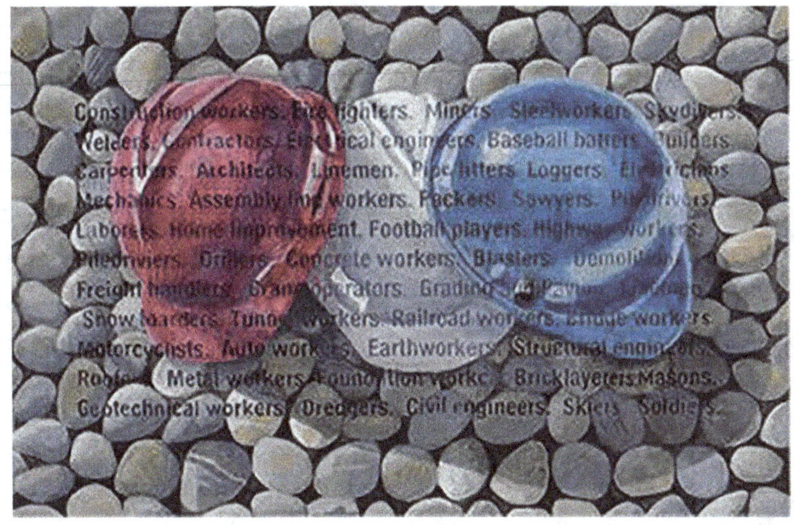

Hard Hats
Watercolor and pastel
29 × 23
2008

Mr. Hardhat

I always thought it was vaguely patriotic to drill, pave, roof, wire, hammer, and basically, sweat for a living.

Among my high school friends in Scarsdale, New York, this was considered a nonstarter. After all, every entitled brainiac from this affluent village should presumably be accepted at Columbia, Princeton, or Washington University (ironically considered a safety school from this egghead district). If one of my classmates ended up with something less than a law degree, they were automatically categorized as unmotivated or something worse ("Wow, are there really such dullards in Scarsdale?").

I never saw myself as a Wall Street lawyer. My high school counselors pushed hard for a SUNY school ("Hey, you might actually get accepted there!"). Under some pressure from the district and my father, who was a successful architect in Manhattan, I decided to enroll in a college but not some artsy-fartsy liberal arts school in Maine. No, my choice was the Ridley-Lowell Business and Technical Institute in Poughkeepsie. After quizzing my dad about the most valuable trade on building sites, his instant answer was convincing. "The electricians have a skill that no one else knows. It's a little mysterious and specialized to all the other construction tradespeople. Hell, I'm not even sure I understand how all those positive and negative electrons work. That's why I hire specialists to do that."

So while others studied psychology 101, public speaking, and fraternity-party planning, I studied electricity. I learned about layout, design and maintenance of every electrical system from homes to high-rises. I loved it! Suffice it to privately say, I did well. As a result, I earned a choice three-year apprenticeship in one of NYC's busiest electrical firms.

"Shit, you can get a real college degree in that amount of time," Bradley Quinn, one of my high school buddies said, not quite realizing that there was an inherent put-down in his comparison.

"Yeah, except I like what I'm doing," I gently shot back. "Besides, beginning next year, I begin earning money." That shut him up as it would anyone in moneygrubbing Scarsdale. Granted, it was only 40 percent what I would eventually make as a fully licensed electrician, but it was not the $50,000 outlay all my friends (and their parents) were paying to Bates, Colby, Middlebury, Bentley, Williams, and other revered universities of higher learning. (Come to think of it, I rather resent the comparative term *higher* learning.)

By now, most of my high school buddies now have diplomas in sociology, communications, history, and English. Four out of five are now bartenders or telephone solicitors.

After my three-year apprenticeship, I bought a van and started my own business. It's called Mr. Electricity. Since it's based in Scarsdale and serves Harrison, Eastchester, and other affluent Westchester communities (where few homeowners have absolutely any idea how to change a lightbulb), I am now inundated with work. I report to no one. I hate to boast, but in my first year of business, I made over $90,000. Incidentally, I do not rub that in to all my struggling college-educated buddies.

My comparative success is not the point. Hey, I always resented that idiotic comparison in high school.

The bigger issue is what I do. I make heat for people. I provide light. In a blackout, I get them off eighteen burning candles on their breakfast island. I connect their off-line computers to the daily info needs of a modern world. Sometimes, I come at midnight to a crying homeowner and reconnect an entire family to the outside world.

I did so last night to my friend Bradley. "Can you repair our devastating outage?" he frantically asked. I was there in twenty minutes, wearing my red, white, or blue hard hat. It was eighty-dollars an hour, but no one cared. Within the next thirty minutes, my high school buddy was again e-mailing his résumés for a job interview that he so sincerely hoped would somehow miraculously come to fruition.

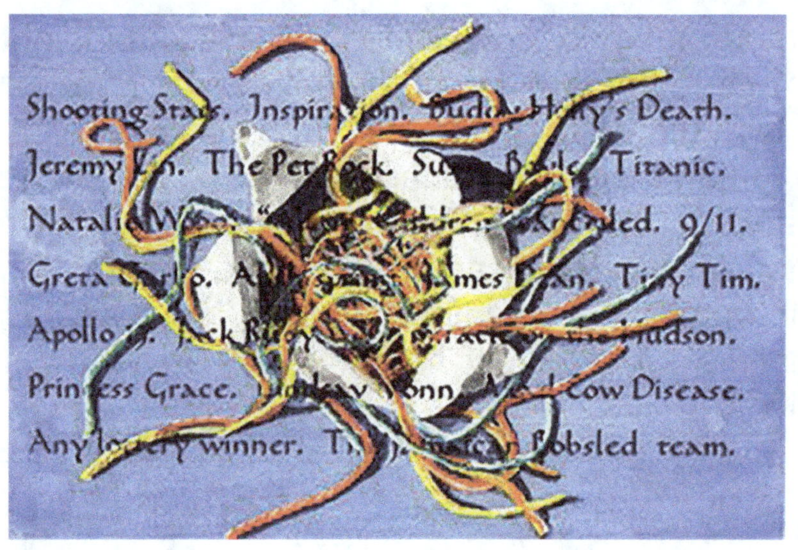

Out of the Blue
Watercolor
23 × 19
2013

Out of the Blue

On July 20, 2012, a young man named James Holmes went into a movie theater in Aurora, Colorado, and indiscriminately shot and killed twelve people. A few years earlier, on the Virginia Tech campus, a student named Cho Seung-Hui shot dead thirty-two unsuspecting people. A few years before that, in Columbine, Colorado, two boys named Eric Harris and Dylan Klebold slaughtered thirteen innocent high school students.

Other than death and gun violence, the incidents had one other thing in common: the instant, explicable motivation.

"His behavior is completely out of the blue," one neighbor remarked about the Aurora mass murderer.

"Who could possibly see this coming?" a Virginia Tech student wondered.

"Who knew?" a Columbine teacher asked at the time.

As a detective in the Bronx, I knew otherwise. There are a few things you quickly learn in this field. Coincidences rarely occur. Also, most things do not happen out of thin air. True, some pedestrian can get blindsided by a car and die. But most of the time, when one person perpetrates a crime against another, there is a rationale. It could be very twisted. Sometimes, you have to unravel a lot of threads to get there. But it's usually there . . . somewhere, just beneath the surface.

I was hoping that would be the case with the murder of the seamstress named Maria Fiorino in Fordham Park, New York. After all, why would anyone want to stab a fifty-seven-year-old woman who sewed wedding dresses for the past twenty-six years for a largely Italian clientele?

"Angela, that's why you are on the case," my precinct captain answered.

The *New York Post*, of course, had a field day with headlines. "Shear revenge?" "Tailor-made slaying!" "So many weddings and a funeral!"

As usual, forensics is a good place to start finding the truth. For the squeamish reader, I do not wish to gross you out, but the victim was stabbed with pinking shears. This narrows things. It was either the seamstress's instrument or that of a competitor in the business.

Next thread? Who had motive? Who were the clients? It only took about four days to knit this mystery together. Evidently, Maria and a company named Belissimo Wedding Gowns had entries from a certain young woman named Anna Gorini.

At this point, my tummy tells me it's just a matter of a few more interviews. Anna admits that she was pitting one wedding dress firm against the other (no crime there). With a subpoena of their books, it's clear that Belissimo Wedding Gowns is one inch from bankruptcy. Witnesses saw Mr. Belissimo enter Maria's shop the evening of the murder. Video cameras on the street confirm this intrusion with a time line that corresponds with Maria's demise.

Then things start to unfurl and connect in a drumroll:

A few more interrogations. A few more gotchas.

Lawyers. Plea bargains.

Charges. First degree.

It's not always this easy. But the sad fact is, most of the time, it is not much more complicated. Somebody has a grudge. Somebody is going down the tubes. Somebody has to pay the ultimate price. None of which will ever bring Maria Fiorino back to life or comfort her children or neighbors.

Of course, there is no headline celebrating the quick resolution by the NYPD of this brutal murder. It's buried on page 10. Ironically, on the front page, there is a screaming headline of a mass murder in Miami. The subhead reads, "An act out of the blue."

As someone who has been at the vortex of these jumbled leads, I instinctively knew that was probably not the case. However, it was also not my precinct. Good luck, Miami.

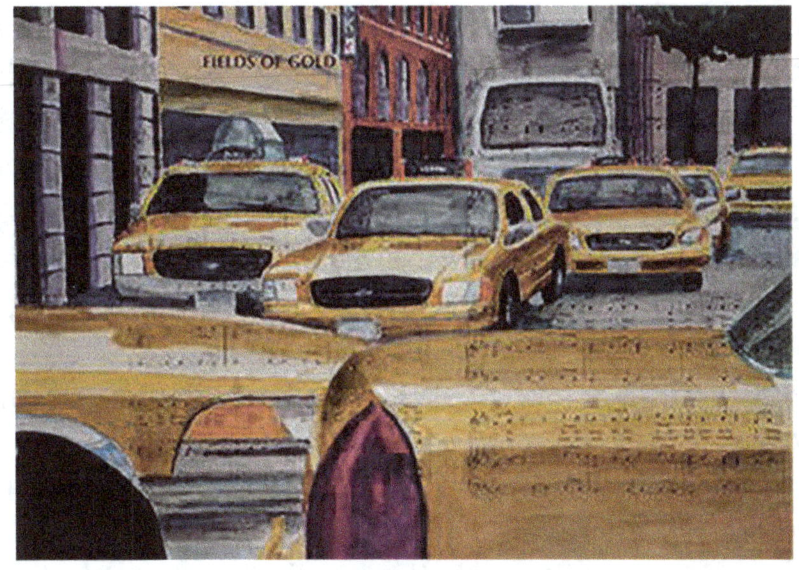

Fields of Gold
Watercolor
30 × 24
2004

Gridlock

"For God's sake, can't you get there any quicker?" Sara Bernstein impatiently barked at the driver after banging on the bulletproof plastic partition that isolates the front section from the passenger seat. The young woman looked at the stalled traffic in every direction and then at the taxi driver's license. "Hello? Hello there! I'm in a bit of a hurry . . . Ached." She fumed, adding the man's Pakistani name, hoping it might miraculously open up a free lane.

"It's five p.m., lady. Rush hour!" The man shrugged and held up his hands like a Borscht belt comedian.

Sara knew it was 5:00 p.m. To be more precise, after looking at her Movado, she knew it was 5:03. And she was supposed to be across town in exactly twelve minutes to meet with her lawyer, Andy Banks. This was at least the fifteenth go-around on the subject. Consequently, it was not a meeting she relished, just one more she wanted over.

"Did you see that?" she squealed to the taxi driver after again knocking on the plastic dividing wall. "You let that cab pull right in front of you. You've got to be a little more aggressive. Otherwise, we'll be stuck in this traffic all day."

Achmed just shook his head. In the course of any day, he would get this sort of backseat driver at least a few times. Normally, he would just ignore the taunt, but today had taken its toll. So he knocked on the partition to mimic her impatience and pointed to his right. "That's the taxi that got ahead of us? Take a look at him now. Stuck behind a truck. Ha!" The driver did another Henny Youngman shrug and then added, "Lady, as my kids like to tell me, you got to chill. We'll get there when we get there."

Sara's initial instinct was to rebut this insubordinate assertion, but the taxi driver was technically correct. Besides, the woman needed to save her composure for Mr. Banks and her ire for her estranged husband and his lawyer.

It was tiresome going through these divorce negotiations. In what has now become increasingly more commonplace, Sara was the major breadwinner in the relationship. Brad, her seldom-hired actor husband, wanted what women of the fifties and sixties wanted: lots of money to "rebuild" a life. The past three months had been a back-and-forth legal struggle. Just when Sara thought all the t's were crossed and the i's were dotted (and she had thought that several times in the past few months), there were always repeated snags.

"He claims he sold his Saab three years ago at your request and wants to be reimbursed for that."

"He wants to know if you will factor in the money he has advanced for this year's vacation."

"Now he claims that you had once promised to cover his old student loans."

At a standstill on Fifty-Third and Sixth Avenue at 5:18, Sara pulled out her cell phone and called Andy Banks. "I'm five blocks away from your office, but the traffic is an absolute parking lot. It may take me twenty minutes."

"No need to hurry," the lawyer reassured her.

Of course not, just like my taxi, the waiting time just gets added to my bill, she thought. "Is there something to sign?" she said with some sincere hope in
her voice.

"Well, that's the thing, Sara. Given the delays, he wants you to reassess the value of the condo on Eighty-Ninth and the weekend house in the Poconos."

There was at least a five-second pause. Involuntarily, Sara sunk deeper in the backseat of the taxi. As Achmed tried to slip ahead of a slow-moving passenger car, he looked in the rearview mirror and couldn't help but see the woman, who appeared on the verge of tears.

"What's this mean? Three weeks? Four weeks? More?" Sara braced herself for the answer.

Her sympathetic lawyer sighed and repeated the question. "What's this mean? Gridlock."

"Perfect," Sara said, looking out the window of the jam-packed, chockablock traffic.

"Get here when you get here," Mr. Banks advised on the cell phone as Sara clicked it off without a response.

Achmed moved three feet forward, then yielded to an angry Mercedes driver to his left, then darted forward, then slammed on his brakes to avoid hitting an oblivious suburbanite in an SUV. In view of the stops and starts and understanding his passenger's earlier pique, Achmed gently knocked on the partition and asked, "Lady, do you want me to cut over to Fifty-Sixth and cut back at Lexington?"

Finally accepting the gridlock and knowing full well that the alternative route would not be faster, just more expensive, Sara Bernstein shrugged like a Catskill comedian and said, "Achmed, chill. When we arrive, we arrive. Whenever."

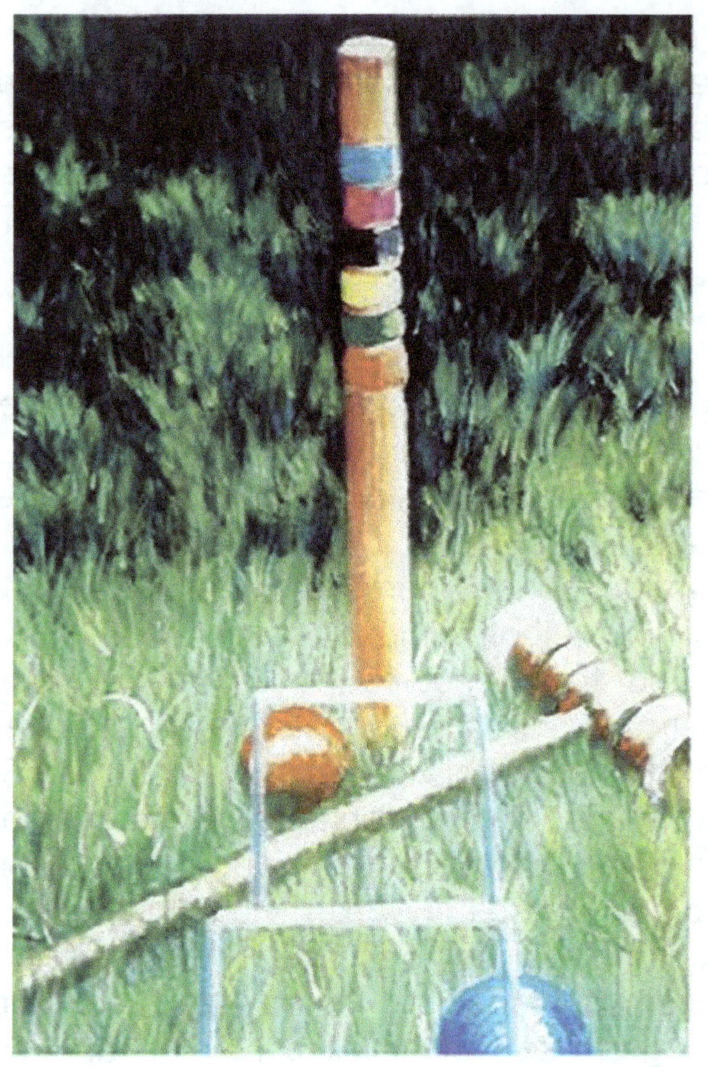

Croquet
Pastel
18 × 24
2003

The Mallet Club Made Modern

In a world of kickboxing, BASE jumping, and hang gliding, the genteel sport of croquet has definitely lost some of its luster. However, Blair Browning Jr., newly appointed president of the Westhampton Mallet Club in Westhampton Beach, New York, was intent on changing the club's appeal and demographics. True, most of the Mallet Club players were women. But they were not the women most men in their twenties or thirties wanted to meet. The vast majority were dowagers in their seventies. And the vast majority of these septuagenarians were the kind that would admonish guests if they were not dressed properly (i.e., white cotton shirt and white pants with cuffs).

Yes, you might advise, "Why bother? Hey, the sport [game?] is what it is—a pastime of another century." As the younger generation likes to say these days, "Hey, you can perfume the pig, but it's still a pig."

President Blair (as the Westhampton members liked to call him) found himself forced to search for some perfume, or at least aftershave. Three days after his election as the top official of the club, the Westhampton Beach city officials wrote him an official letter about the continuation of the decades-long tradition of Saturday morning matches at Cox's Field.

"Given the fact that that this is a community property, we must do our best to accommodate all our constituents—coed volleyball teams, gut Frisbee tournaments, chili cook-offs, roller hockey leagues—all of which require use of Cox's field. It has come to our attention that there is scant attendance at your croquet outings on Saturday mornings. Unless you can indicate extenuating circumstances by September 25, we must reluctantly readjust our scheduling to the more popular events and ask you to please consider a different destination for your weekly croquet tournaments."

As is the case with most messages in the Hamptons, it was worded gently and nicely, but the knife was ready to plunge. However, Blair Browning Jr. was not about to have the demise of the Westhampton Mallet Club happen on his watch.

Within three days, he called the fifteen lifelong members together for an emergency meeting. Rather than assault the members with this ticking time bomb, Blair decided to ease his way into this topic. "Elizabeth, when did you join our wonderful club?" "Anna, what about you?" "Frances? Katherine?"

"Nineteen sixty-three." "Nineteen sixty-seven." "Nineteen seventy-one." "Nineteen sixty-four." Over the next fifteen minutes, Blair spoke about the good old days. Then he threw out a bit of shock therapy.

"A few years before you all joined us, JFK was assassinated, Kent State happened, and we went to the moon. The world changed. And it has changed again over the last decade."

Thirty minutes later, after all the members complained about the lack of elegance in today's world, Blair hit them with the cold, hard fact. "Unless, we can get several hundred people out to Cox's Field next month, we will be playing croquet in the alley forever."

Facing the death of an institution, the women panicked. Blair then presented his prerehearsed four-point plan:

1. The dress code must be relaxed. Anyone under thirty was encouraged to wear a bikini.
2. Long Island iced tea would be scrumptiously served to all participants.
3. All the young fraternity boys from Southampton College would be invited, partly induced by new rule no. 2, but more likely rule no. 4.
4. All the women were to invite their nieces, daughters, and granddaughters, provided they adhered to rule no. 1.

Reluctantly, all the septuagenarians agreed to the game plan and showed up the following Saturday. So did the young women and the thirsty boys from college. On the first week's match, two hundred people attended. The following week, there were 230 participants. The next week, 245 bikini-clad, Long Island iced tea–imbibing contestants.

Fortunately, seventy-four-year-old Elizabeth Roberts won the nine-wicket contest. Thanks to Blair Browning's PR savvy, she was photographed in her dress whites, holding a trophy, surrounded by several young men in their Speedos and several women in bikinis, all holding up red plastic cups.

Last week, in front of the city council, the Westhampton Mallet Club's hold on Cox's Field was renewed for the remainder of the summer. The roller hockey league has been reassigned to Montauk and is considering playing in dress whites.

They are thinking of adding wickets to their asphalt field. Just last night, one parent suggested an alternative ploy: playing in bikinis for Long Island iced tea. As of now, it is under consideration. If I were a betting person, I would wager they would eventually learn the lesson of the Mallet Club.

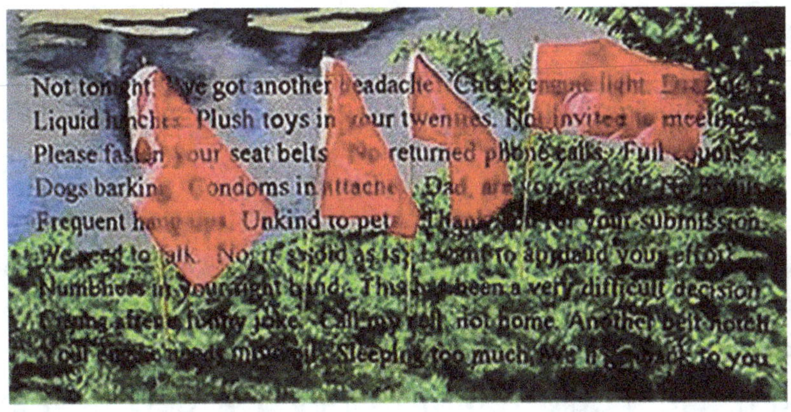

Red Flags
Watercolor
30 × 18
2007

Red Flags

In the early years of their marriage, Bonnie Carlyle had never considered herself the suspicious type. However, in the past few months, there were certain telltale signs that suggested that her husband of twenty-two years might again be cheating on her.

The first clue was that Joel had begun to regularly get home at one, two, or three in the morning. "It's our big sales season," he pleaded. When his wife called his office after nine or ten, there was never an answer. According to Joel, he had to turn off his cell phone during those late hours rather than interrupt sales meetings.

After a few weeks of complaints, the man did curtail his late-night sales calls for about six days. But then he resumed his after-midnight schedule and informed Bonnie that it was the only way to keep his business growing.

There were other equally concrete indications: the lipstick smear on his undershorts, the condoms in his attaché, and of course, the lack of libido in
the bedroom.

These kinds of dalliances had occurred in their marriage every year or two. The first time, it took Bonnie some months to recognize the red flags (they were more muted in those early days). However, she was now quite practiced at reading the signs. Unfortunately, over the years, he had also learned how to deflect her suspicions with one far-fetched excuse or another.

Yes, it was a dishonest relationship on both of their parts. Joel's behavior required true acting skills. But Bonnie had dissembled as well. She had lived with the falsehoods and had not taken action. As her therapist told her a decade ago, "This is a form of mental cruelty, you know. And you can change that by leaving." There were three reasons she never did. After the usual three-month fling, Joel would typically return. He would return to being a decent father. And he would resume being a good provider.

Those last two were now in a state of flux. By now, the children were safely away at college. And just this year, Joel's company went public, quadrupling his already significant wealth. In terms of money, flux was an understatement.

Consequently, Bonnie decided that enough was enough. Instead of going back to her therapist, who would undoubtedly remind her, "Hey, I told you so," she instead went to a private investigator who promised that he could photographically capture proof of those vivid, crimson-red flags.

I know, this turn of events must make Bonnie seem like a gold digger. But let's face facts: she was the injured party. His affairs had occurred at least ten times over two decades. Now in her late forties, Bonnie reasoned that those trysts might now happen more frequently. Why endure it? And if not now, when?

The pictures from the PI were hurtful but conclusive. The woman on Joel's arm was in her twenties. (Evidently, her name was Amber.) There were photos of the two of them in restaurants, in his BMW convertible, and outside her apartment, including one with Joel in his undershorts and Amber topless.

It was enough to finally spur Bonnie to action. She bought four large
red envelopes.

In one she put Joel's lipstick-smudged boxer shorts. She wrote the note: "Amber's favorite flavor?"

In the next, she put Joel's condom with the note, "Found in your attaché. Glad you are being careful."

In the third, she placed all the copies of the photographs from her private eye and the note, "I don't think the kids would love to see these."

In the last envelope, she placed the business card of her divorce lawyer with the message, "Probably too bad for you we don't have a prenup."

Oh, and one more thing: she bought four crimson flags, which she placed by the front pond of their mansion. With a slightest breeze, they unfurled and were quite attractive. Just for good measure, she also added spotlights on each so they could be clearly visible late at night.

When the smug and sexually satiated Joel Carlyle drove up the long driveway and saw the red flags at 2:15 a.m., he found the display curious. Once he sneaked into the kitchen, his curiosity was answered. He picked up the paper on the island and read the cryptic note, "It took me a long time to see the red flags. I trust you saw them all tonight."

He then looked at the four red envelopes and returned to the note. "Read all four. Especially number 4. He is waiting for your call tomorrow."

Bonnie had heard the kitchen door open ten minutes ago. She too had learned how to act. And yet, the smile on her face was mixed with some wet eyes. That's the effect of twenty-two years. However, once she wiped her tears on the pillow, the smile still endured and became stronger with every solo hour.

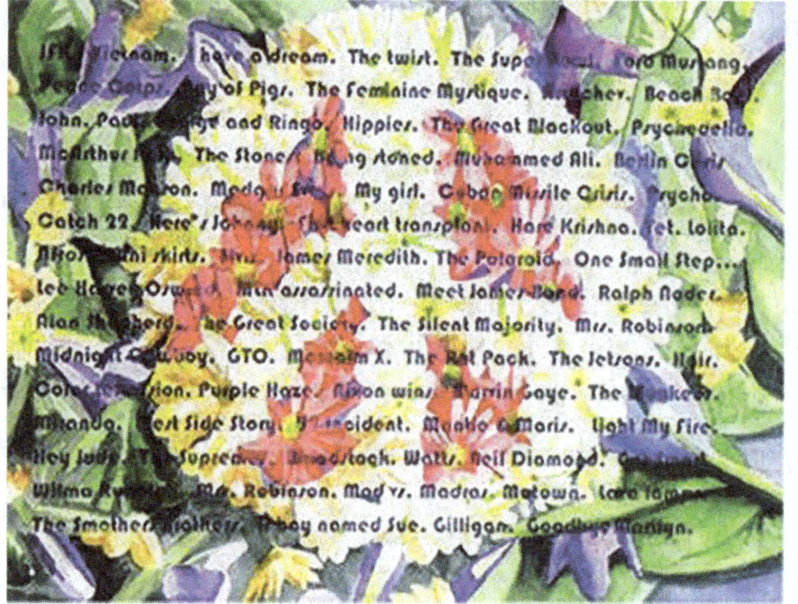

The Sixties,
Watercolor
32 × 25
2010

Where Have All the Flowers Gone?

Where have all the flowers gone? Long time passing.
Where have all the flowers gone? Long time ago.
Where have all the flowers gone? Girls have picked them every one.
When will they ever learn? When will they ever learn?

—Pete Seeger

In 1960, Mr. Seeger's anthem to peace became a surprisingly meaningful folk hit for the decade. As JFK, RFK, MLK, and others were brutally slain, the wistful nature of the song became even more poignant. As Cambodia, Vietnam, and even Kent State seemed to build a mountain of body bags, the plea of the song was all the more heartbreaking, especially for peaceniks like Marc Driscoll.

Marc had escaped the draft with a high lottery number. It was a lucky draw for the young man; otherwise, he would have ended up in Canada. Instead, he was able to demonstrate with other stop-the-war activists and fully participate in American society.

Other than the dark side of the decade, there were things to appreciate: an explosion of creativity, women's liberation, a race to the moon. As a young engineer, Marc Driscoll had actually joined this NASA endeavor and was in the Houston control room when Neil Armstrong uttered his "One small step" phrase.

Ironically, thanks to his involvement in this mission, Marc Driscoll would forever be dubbed a patriot. "It was a just a job," he once explained to the local newspaper, but that truth only translated to the outside world as patriotic humility. Everyone in his family admired him, including his only son, Patrick, who often asked his dad to come to grade school and talk about the moon launches. Reluctantly, Mr. Driscoll did agree, and that led to an address to the entire district assembly (including parents)—more publicity, more groundbreaking American accolades.

In the context of all this (and since sons do sometimes view their fathers as role models), Patrick hoped to someday do something as meaningful for America. On his twentieth birthday, young Patrick enlisted in the marines and volunteered to go to Afghanistan. That afternoon, he proudly announced it to his dad.

"No! You can't be serious," Mr. Driscoll instantly protested.

"I thought you'd be proud of me," the young boy retorted.

"You know I hate this war! It's like Vietnam all over again!"

"It's my way to fight for our freedoms. Just like you did, Dad."

"No, I didn't. I pushed a few buttons and looked at some graphs, and a man got to the moon! Period! I wasn't holding a gun."

Back and forth. Back and forth. Back and forth. Fact is, it's next to impossible to forbid a twenty-year-old to do something he truly feels is his once-in-a-lifetime chance to stand for something bigger than himself. And in a rather subliminal way, isn't that how he was raised?

It has now been eleven months on this latest tour of duty. It is Patrick's second stint in the Kandahar Province.

Every morning, Mr. Driscoll gets up at 5:30 a.m. and checks the latest international news on CNN. He pays special attention to the casualties in Afghanistan and holds his breath when the reports are released. He's an intelligent man, and he can tell that things seem to be going haywire over there. He hates to think about it. So he goes to mass every morning at 7:00 a.m. and says a prayer.

So far, so good. His son will be released in one month. Just like the moon launch, he counts the days—thirty, twenty-nine, twenty-eight . . .

On his way to work, he sometimes listens to hits from his favorite decade. Just this morning, he heard "Where Have All the Flowers Gone?" Yes, suddenly it felt like the 1960s all over again.

Five, four, three, two . . .

"When will they ever learn? When will they ever learn?"

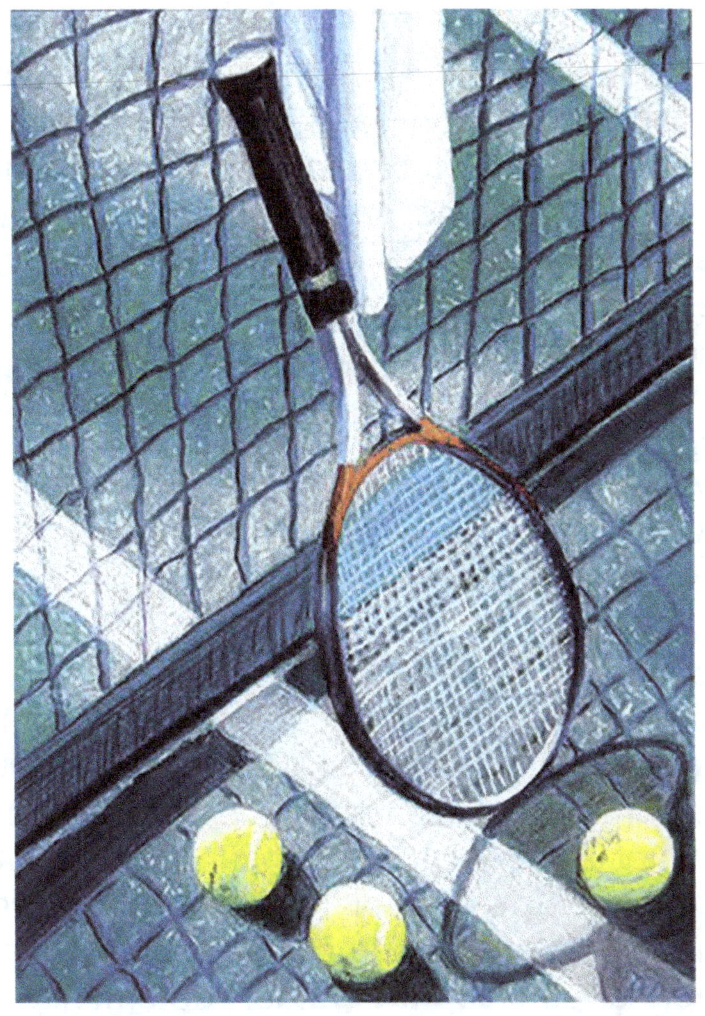

Love One

Ever since Chris Woodward had picked up a tennis racket at age five, he had been taught to aggressively play to win. "Go for the angles! Don't play it safe! If you're afraid to lose, you will never win," his father often told him.

As is true with most father/instructors, Warren Woodward's relationship with his son was complicated. On the one hand, he admired the kid's innate talent.

In addition, he was pleased with his son's work ethic and his ability to control temper tantrums (something the father always struggled with in his playing days).

However, the boy's occasional inability to "stand on the gas and slam the door shut on a victory" always bothered Mr. Woodward. "If you are ahead in a match, you cannot give your opponent one single inch. After all, this is a game of momentum. Give it up, and you become a loser."

When these critical thoughts entered Mr. Woodward's head, he tried to remind himself that young Chris was now only thirteen. Undoubtedly, the boy would learn the value of unrelenting grit through match play. He would inevitably feel some matches turn. Hopefully, it would all dawn on him next year. That's when young Chris would be playing competitive matches at Palm Beach High School, and he would very likely be ranked in the national top-thirty under-fifteen category.

As Mr. Woodward completely understood from his own once-promising career, at this point, it becomes a head game. Every top-fifty player has near-equal athletic skills. The will to win, the need to prevail, and the urgency to dismantle, destroy, and humiliate one's opponent are what separate the potential pros from the also-rans. For that reason, forty-five-year-old Warren Woodward decoded it was time to change his son's instruction regimen. This year, instead of nonstop ground strokes, the father determined that his son needed to be game-tough. There is an easy, nonconfrontational way to do this: play points. Chris serves ten, and you play out the points. Then Dad serves ten, and you play out those points. However, it's not a real game. And at this level, Mr. Woodward instinctively knew there was nothing like a real game.

For the last forty days, the father and son had played these mock matches. As a nationally ranked player in his twenties and a wily veteran, Mr. Woodward clearly had the early advantage. Most sets would end up 6–2 or 6–3. Lately, however, the matches had tightened and more frequently ended 6–4.

"One of these days, the kid is going to beat me," Mr. Woodward told the club pro at the Palm Beach Country Club. "Well, you should hope so," the club pro honestly answered. "Otherwise, he will never get in the top ten."

It was a brutal truth. On an intellectual level, the father knew the day would eventually come when the kid would outrun, outplay, and outpoint him. Mr. Woodward figured it might happen when the kid was fifteen. But at thirteen? Hard to swallow since he had never lost to his son.

That was about to happen in today's practice session. The son was ahead 5–3 and serving for the match. After a miffed return of serve, Mr. Woodward slammed his racket into the Har-Tru court as he had done when he blew that junior match thirty years ago against Andre Agassi.

Chris silently watched the childish display and then looked to the sky while his dad retrieved his racket. Once his father had it in hand, the boy took a deep, thoughtful breath and then repeatedly bounced the ball before his next serve. From that moment, the tide turned, and the dad rolled off four straight games to carry the set.

"What happened?" Mr. Woodward asked his son, acting as if he really wanted to know.

"You simply rose to the challenge," the son quietly told his father/instructor.

Something inside his young man's heart told him that this was not the right day to dethrone his dad. It was enough to know that at thirteen, he now had the skills to do so. It wasn't really an act of pity, more an act of love to the one man who had devoted so much to his son's success.

By the way, it would never happen again. As Mr. Woodward observed in every one of his son's college matches, the young man never choked. As Chris noted from that day forth, his father always decided it was best to just practice ground strokes.

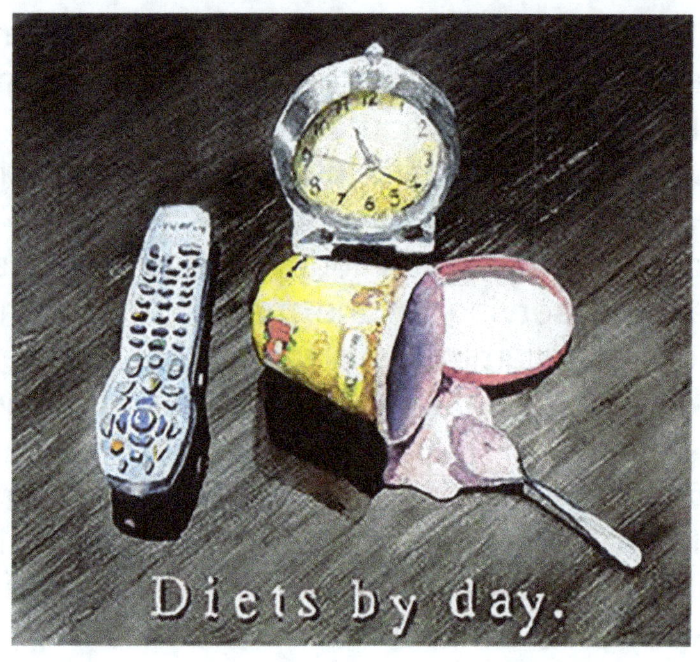

Diets by Day
Watercolor
30 × 23
2013

Diets by Day

I have tried eighteen crash diets. I do pilates twice a week. I ride a stationary bicycle three times a week. I have tried Weight Watchers, the Atkins diet, the Scarsdale, Beverly Hills, and Malibu diets, and I am still twenty pounds over the ideal weight to be mindlessly boffed on the spur of the moment.

Oh, and one more thing: I am really tired of living a life of virtue. I know, I know. I have heard about the zen high that supposedly inhabits your soul once you accept a life of regularity, regimen, and consistent results. However, I have never once experienced this so-called elevated state of being. And come to think of it, where is the goddamn sponteneity? When people talk about this meditative *Ohhhm* sensation, they never mention the word *fun*.

My theory? If we're gonna aim for balance, I vote for equal measures of early-morning aerobic sweat and late-night Häagen-Dazs. Admittedly, this is not the ideal way to trim those extra twenty (OK, twenty-five) pounds. But it does lead to some sense of serenity before the midnight cable news loops begin repeating themselves. And it can lead to sex.

Perhaps it is time to introduce myself. My name is Marsha Woodbine. As I have described myself on a few too many dating sites, "I am a Manhattan professional woman in my thirties, independent, curvy [a well-known euphemism on most dot.coms], independent, happy with my own self, but also craving something forbidden late at night."

At the time, I used to include a very accurate picture of myself in a Wall Street business suit, juxtaposed with jammies on the sofa. Consequently, I was inundated with requests. Yes, some were fatties, but most were not! The vast majority were NYC lawyers and day traders looking for something different. I began to include a few of my like-minded friends. I supplemented that with some guys who did not want to go out with Stepford-wife surrogates. But I could not keep up with the outragous demand.

And so, I created the business. If you watch TV after midnight on some cable channels, you have probably seen my commercials. I use the exhibited, decadent picture tagged "Diets by Day," and then go to black—with the title card that communicates, "Who know what by night?"

Häagen-Dazs has just threatened to sue me. By now, as a multimillion dollar company, I have my own Manhattan lawyers, and of course, they have countersued. Their argument? "Hey, Häagen-Dazs, you lost *zero* business [moreover, you have increased your business in Manhattan by 30 percent]. Come to think of it, shouldn't we sue for profits? Should we not claim a percentage of increased gains? Should we not do a victory lap?"

Privately, I have agreed to "Just move forward." (Between the lines, that means no one wins or loses, i.e., let's drop this damn unwinnable case.) Chances are, you heard that on the *Today* show this morning.

News flash! It was just reported that the average American is thirty pounds overweight. This is nationwide. This is nonreversible. This has implications for all drug companies, all weight-loss scams, all insurance companies, and only one website connection site.

The name of the winning site is Diets by Day. If you fit the bill, just type http://www.dietsbyday.com.

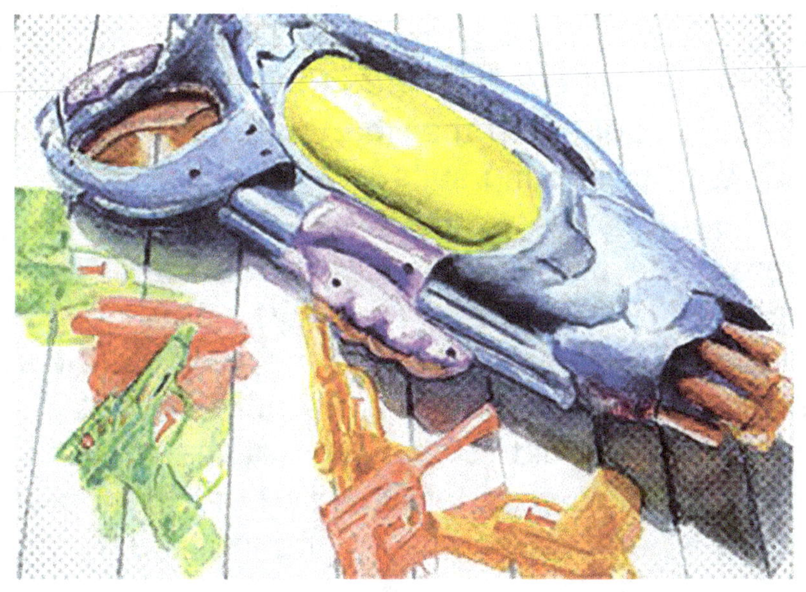

Davids vs. Goliath
Watercolor
18 × 14
2013

David, David, Davids versus Goliath

"This is so cool," Mr. Margolies gushed like a kid when he opened up the new superpowered water rifle.

"Arnold, remember, this is a game," Annie Margolies cautioned her type A husband. "You know your job is to get soaked by all the boys. Not the other

way around."

Her husband, holding the multicolored rifle, took imaginary aim at a tree. He then winked at his wife. "This is going to be so much fun," he answered noncommittally.

The event was young David Margolies's birthday. The seven-year-old had been looking forward to it for the past three months. As he had discovered a few years back, it was nice to have a birthday in August—when the sun was shining, the pool was open, and all his friends were happy to have one last blast before the new school year.

This year, his mom and dad promised David a memorable water-soaked celebration. They had added a basketball rim to the backyard pool and suggested that the young boy invite twelve of his favorite friends with swimming suits.

At this time, perhaps it's worth explaining that both Mr. and Mrs. Margolies were party planners by day. As a result, an invitation to one of their parties (even their son's party) was a coveted ticket. No one ever said no. Everyone knew that there would always be some fully integrated, creative surprise at a Margolies event.

For example, Annie couldn't help but set the mood with the rain-soaked invitation sent to each of David's best friends. In the goody bag, she packed a personalized towel and individual water pistols for each kid.

It was that colorful assortment of plastic pistols that inspired a theatrical finale in the mind of Arnold Margolies. "A massive water fight!" the former actor grinned. "I can be the invading commando with my supersized water rifle. It'll be a battle to the finish."

"In the pool?" Annie asked.

"Nah, a water fight is no fun if you're already wet. You gotta be dry! I say we do it after the cake. After the goody bags of water-filled guns."

As soon as all the boys had sung "Happy Birthday," Mr. Margolies excused himself. In the kitchen, he put on some colorful war paint and filled his water rifle with cold water. Then he tiptoed behind the boxwood hedge and watched the kids open up their goody bags.

As Arnold had learned on stage, timing is everything. When one boy took out the water pistol, that was his cue. The commando/dad unleashed a twenty-yard squirt in the general direction of the party.

"Is it raining?" the boy innocently asked.

In came another twenty-yard squirt. This time a few boys reacted to the general direction of the water and looked to the four-foot hedge. After a few seconds, the dad popped his head above the greenery and sent another blast of water toward the seven-year-old boys.

"Attack," young David instantly said to his friends. "Guys, grab your weapons!" Through a gaggle of giggles, all the boys joined the hunt through the backyard. For a while, it was a fair fight with Mr.

Margolies's exploding howitzer of waterpower. However, within two minutes, the swarm was able to surround the dad. In a performance worthy of an Academy Award, Arnold took the shots as if they were bullets and finally succumbed to the onslaught, tossing his water rifle to his son, and then stumbled backward into the pool. Of course, the man was fully clothed in a business suit. Otherwise, what fun would it be?

Three hours later, eight-year-old David Margolies was still giggling. He loved all the gifts from his friends, and the whole day. "That was so cool," David said, holding his new prized water rifle.

"Mom, did you get a picture of Dad falling in the pool?"

"Sure did."

"That was so cool," the kid repeated, echoing his dad's reaction to first holding the colorful rifle.

Instinctively, Mr. and Mrs. Margolies looked at each other, telepathically communicating that their dedication to event planning was, lo and behold, the perfect fit for their personalities.

The eight-year-old then innocently put the water rifle down. "What do we do next year?"

The parents again looked at each other, but now with a unison sigh. On these heels of this extravaganza, both knew they had created a never-ending bar to achieve for the next ten years.

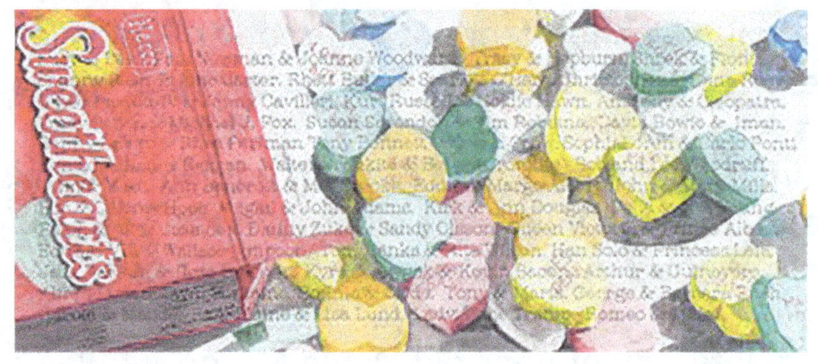

Sweethearts
Watercolor
29 × 17
2007

Sweethearts

I don't like to discuss my marriage, but I will tell you something which may sound corny, but which happens to be true. I have steak at home. Why should I go out for hamburger?

—Paul Newman

In an era when almost one of every two American marriages ends in divorce, the thirty-five-year-old union between Anna and Michael Youngblood was something of an anomaly, especially since both parties had brief affairs, very separate careers, and drastically different backgrounds.

As most of their neighbors in the Santa Fe would privately admit, "They are not a very well art-directed couple . . . but damn, they are fun."

Michael was a full foot taller than his bride and had a far kinder heart than his imposing visage would suggest. As he often liked to joke to tourists, he was 100 percent Navajo and 110 percent smart businessman. This apparent lack of arithmetic did not deter him from becoming the most profitable purveyor of Navajo nation crafts in the town square. As a matter of fact, his large retail shop sat on the eastern corner and was just a few feet from the Santa Fe Cooking School.

That's where Anna—a blond, petite San Francisco native who was originally trained at the French Culinary Institute—now taught every day. Decades ago, she had traded her training in crepes, steak au poivre, and macaroons for blue corn tortillas and any dish that relished the spice of red chilies. "Eating is like sex," she often told her students. "It should be a daily exhilarating thrill."

In their late twenties, the two apparent misfits had somehow landed in a place that likes to advertise itself as "the city different." At the time, Michael was haggling on a rug with one hundred other silversmiths every weekend, and Anna ran a food cart of Les Oeufs de la Ranch.

Eleven months later, they were married. She liked the jewelry the man made and suggested he make golf-oriented cufflinks for tourists and use his charm to bargain better. He proposed she rename her cart Huevos Rancheros a la minute. At first they both laughed at each other's notions. Thirty-four years and three hundred sixty-four days later, they still appreciate each other's ideas and are still laughing.

Yes, they have strayed. Yes, they have fought finances. Yes, they have cried through the difficulty and guilt of bearing no children. But they have something more. It doesn't happen every day, but on many afternoons, their private sense of humor sustains them. Put most simply, thanks to each other, they find a way to smile.

It's a jest.

It's a joust.

It's sarcastic.

It's ironic.

It's humiliating.

It's elevating.

It's what they fear.

It's what they hope.

It's a sense of distance.

It's a sense of personal, private knowledge.

It's wonderful.

It's weird.

Tomorrow, Anna and Michael will have their thirty-fifth anniversary celebration with many close friends at the Coyote Café in Santa Fe.

Tonight will be even more special. Instead of a hamburger dinner, Anna will make her husband a steak au poivre rouge at home. Michael will present a locket he did not buy from the weekly street vendors but instead made of his own hand. They will share the cheap, chalky gifts they exchanged on their first real date. It says "Sweetheart" in a goofy, homey, forever immature way.

They will laugh. And they will laugh. And they will laugh. And they will love. Perhaps even forever.

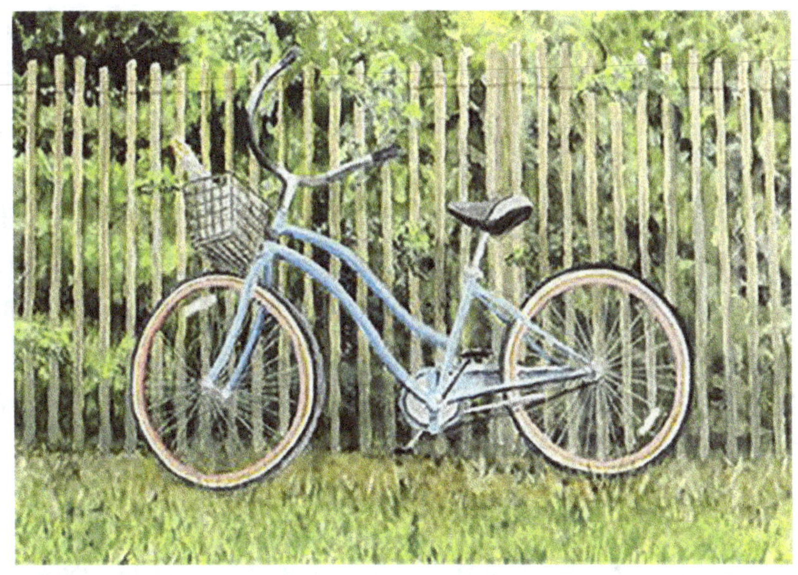

The Daily Commute
Watercolor
22 × 20
2012

The Daily Commute

For thirty-two years, Mary Conrad trudged from her apartment on Eighty-Second and Riverside to the Seventy-Ninth Street station at 6:33 in the morning. Unless there was a huge snowstorm or a late wake-up, she would catch the No. 6 at 6:48 and then race to the Herald Square shuttle at 7:26. If everything worked like clockwork, she would catch the train to Grand Central Shuttle and be in her office at Fortieth and Madison by 8:15 a.m.

It was a routine that paid significant dividends for at least the past twenty-five years. During that time, Mary rose through the ranks of an ad agency called Young & Rubicam. She started in the print production, became the head of that department within a decade, and ended up running all TV, broadcast, and Internet production for Y&R at 285 Madison.

Unlike most agency jobs, it did not require many overnight trips. Like many advertising leadership roles, it paid quite well and afforded stock options. Thanks to this unique combination, Mary was able to save her nickels and help her two sons graduate from the expensive Dalton School three blocks from her home. After that, the older one graduated from Brown University, and the other from

Ithaca College in upstate New York. Both resettled in the New York area and had begun to create their own lives . . . that did not ordinarily include Mom. But as Mary Conrad reassured herself, independence was always the goal.

As a Manhattan empty nester, she hoped that her days ahead would be heaven. After all, at least two hundred thousand people in their fifties move to the Big Apple every year. True, this annual influx is outnumbered by the young and the rushed—hordes of aggressive type A personalities who exit Grand Central every morning and dictate messages into an almost invisible phone mike, reminiscent of crazy people communicating with the clouds.

For months, this electronic mumblings bothered Mary Conrad. However, as one of the acknowledged experts in one-on-one communications, she reluctantly accepted it. What she could not accept was that her agency of thirty-two years went public and was suddenly obsessed with the Wall Street / Dow Jones index. More disturbing, Y&R was soon acquired by a British conglomerate, and fear gripped every employee as new management invaded from across the pond.

Gordon Plimsoll, the twenty-eight-year-old extremely talented upstart from Liverpool interviewed her three weeks later and asked if she was "hungry." Mary answered, "Yes, indeed!" With some flair, she left that afternoon for the Oyster Bar in Grand Central and never returned.

It has now been six months since she sold her Riverside condo and moved to West Hampton. It is not the most exclusive enclave of Long Island, but it is quite tony compared to almost every region of the United States. Her three-bedroom home cost over 750 thousand. It is not on the ocean. It does not have a pool. But it does have easy access to the water (six blocks) and the best homemade bread in the local bakery. At least twice a week, she rides her bike to Josie's bakeshop to pick up a fresh baguette after fully reading the *New York Times*. It's normally around 10:00 a.m., but for the first time in her life, she is not religiously obsessed with the schedule.

Last night, her Brown graduate called and suggested that he and his girlfriend come out for summer weekend. A few minutes later, her

Ithaca boy suggested the same routine. "Wow," she remarked to herself. "Life comes full circle."

Ten minutes later, there was an unexpected call from area code 212. "Mary, the man said, "This is Gordon Plimsoll."

"Wow again," she said, which meant nothing to the young Brit.

"Yes, indeed. We had a brief talk when I first came to Y&R seven months ago." At this point, there was a pause. Mary had no intention of filling the

dead air.

"Yes . . . well, anyway . . . yes. As I assess this department," the young man clumsily pushed forward and then gathered steam. "I feel that your inestimable experience and talents could be quite useful here, and I just wanted to . . ."

His entreaty was interrupted by a hearty laugh from Mary Conrad. In truth, she had hoped that the old place would miss her. However, it was beyond a fantasy that the young upstart would beg her to reconsider. Obviously, he was ordered to get Ms. Conrad back on staff and steady the ship. This comeuppance pleased her all the more.

As nicely as she could, she told the young Brit, "Mr. Plimsoll, I am hungry. Very hungry." She then looked at her watch and observed that it was 9:52. "I have a rather important meeting at 10:00 a.m.-ish, and it unfortunately precludes a continuation of this conversation."

As far as Mary could remember, she had never used the word *preclude* in a telephone conversation, but it felt good to speak the queen's English to the young cockney upstart. It felt even better to get on her baby-blue bike and pedal her way to Josie's bakeshop to get a fresh baguette for the upcoming visit from her two sons.

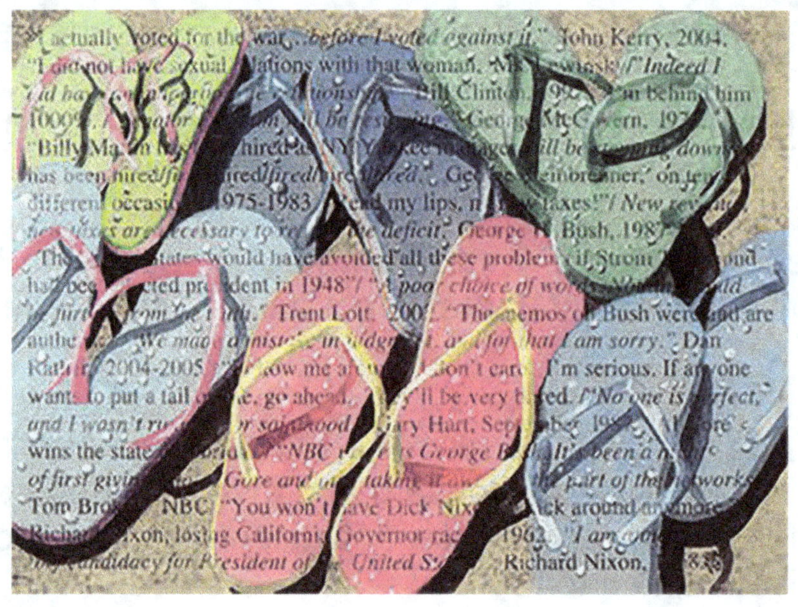

Flip-Flops
Watercolor
29 × 22
2005

The King of Flip-Flops

I don't really believe people choose their sexual orientation. And if so, why would I ever hold that against any individual?

—*Clark Williams III (R-Florida)*

In 1996, it was an unexpected announcement from the man running for the US Senate from the toss-up state of Florida. In truth, it was an answer to a rather limited question as to whether or not he would allow gays and lesbians to serve on his staff if he were elected. It was not intended as a proposal to repeal "Don't Ask, Don't Tell" or change the marriage laws of the Sunshine State.

However, the conservative activists jumped on the senatorial candidate's comment and circulated propaganda that Mr. Clark Williams was far too pro-gay to effectively represent the pro-Christian (and pro-Jewish) state of Florida. It didn't work. Thanks to the man's business endorsements, NRA supports, and benignly moderate social views, he eked out a victory in the primary and easily won in the general election.

As a result, he commanded the cover of *Time* magazine ("The New Face of GOP moderation") and *Newsweek* ("A kinder, gentler

Republican"). After a cakewalk reelection in 2002, the national beltway press almost always included him in the inner circle of possible GOP candidates for the presidential race of 2008. His marriage two years earlier to Mary Keene, the middle-aged daughter of a Tampa Baptist minister, helped shore up his conservative base. The senator's revised right-wing views on a variety of issues also contributed to his conservative appeal.

Examples:

Abortion (1994: "It's a decision between a woman and her god." 2008: "It's a sin against nature.")

Affirmative Action (1994: "Everyone deserves an equal chance at success." 2008: "You can never have equality by giving minorities special privileges.")

Immigration Reform (1994: "I believe in the Statue of Liberty's promise." 2008: "We need to build a bigger wall between Mexico and the US border.")

Despite some critics who called his current positions "complete 100 percent reversals of his core beliefs," his advisors loved the upward spiral of his research numbers. However, that benignly pro-gay comment haunted them. "Can you not just come out again in 2008 and call it another 'sin against nature'?"

"Nope, it's only 5 percent of the vote and not worth the flip-flop," the presidential candidate pushed back.

By the third national debate, when he was tagged by the Tea Party candidates as "Easy on gays," "Pro–sex change operations," and allowing gay and lesbian teachers to openly admit their sexual orientation to grade school students (when asked), Clark Williams III clearly understood the pressure of his inflexible position.

In his third debate, he waited for an assault from his opponents and then responded, "I believe in the Bible. And Jesus, while he never specifically spoke against gays, was obviously against same-gender relationships, as am I . . . as I read the Bible."

It took about thirty seconds for his opponents to pounce on the once-frontrunner Clark Williams III.

"So you compare yourself to Jesus," Michelle Barynski (R-WI) accused.

"So you have completely flip-flopped on your position of 1994," Robert Stone (R-LA) chimed.

"So you think Jesus was cowardly and noncommittal on the subject?" (Jesse Monroe, R-Utah).

Within three weeks of damage control, Clark Williams III announced that he was suspending his presidential quest to reassess "current opportunities." He was not invited to speak at the GOP convention. In fact, he was absent from all the major news programs coverage. In the first two years of the Obama administration, this once fair-haired candidate disappeared. As a matter of fact, his divorce from Mary Keene, the daughter of the Baptist minister, was barely reported in any media.

However, the paparazzi-covered photos of Clark Williams III and his young male companion walking in swim shorts and flip-flops along the Key West beach commanded many covers in the *National Inquirer, National Globe*, and *Tattler.*

"Mr. Williams, does this behavior signify a flip-flop on your statement at the Republican debates?" one reporter barked within earshot.

Clark asked his partner to stop and then addressed the paparazzi. "I refer you to my statement of 1996, which I have never denied. And if that's not enough, go fuck yourself!" He then grabbed his partner's hand, and the two men walked away from the interrogating crowd. It was the last anyone heard of Clark Williams.

Opening night. Job interview. First date.
Meeting the parents. Audition. SAT results.
College acceptance. Grades posted tonight.
New business pitch. Offer on a condominium.
Your verdict. State championship game.
Sudden death. Overtime. Photo finish.
Extra innings. Spelling bee. The jury is out.
Will you marry me? We have your prognosis.
I am pleased to announce that the winner is....

Pins and Needles (and Lola)

In the next ten minutes, Sophia Senna would know her fate. She had meticulously crafted the elegant designs and rehearsed the girls for their runway performance. ("Chin up," she told one model. "Look down your nose at the people below as if they are all your subjects, and you are the king.") Soon, there would be a thunderous, welcoming applause or a tepid and "nice try / better luck next year" response.

Either way, it would have consequences for Ms. Senna. For years, the fashionista had high hopes for her debut as a stand-alone designer. As a matter of fact, most of her fans and reporters had felt she had stayed far too long as Domenico Dolce's premiere designer.

"Sophia, why exhaust all your talent for another one's fame?" Karl Lagerfeld once told her. "Come work for me. I'll put your name on the label . . . just below mine."

The Dior family had made overtures to give her the freedom to revamp their entire line, again with their name first.

The Bendel boutique had given her the greatest push. Henri Bendel, the owner of the fashion fortress on Fifty-Seventh Street in Manhattan, had promised her "an exclusive prime retail spot, provided you have good reviews in Milano . . . which I assume you will achieve with creativity and surprise."

Ahh, those two conjoined, bedeviling challenges!

Let's put it this way, Sophia Senna could design dresses in her sleep. Sheer, innate talent was never an issue. Risk was. Perhaps that's why she had stayed with Dolce & Gabbana so many years. There was a predictable, soft, feminine mystique about the place—part of the brand. The colors would change. The flow would be adjusted. The overall aura would move twenty, maybe even forty, degrees. Sophia was always on the outer edge of forty degrees, and that's why Domenico Dolce valued her. (Incidentally, when she announced her desire to go it alone, he smiled and encouraged her to "break new boundaries. Otherwise, why leave?")

Finally, at this debut unveiling of her signature style, she did so. Unlike her taffeta dresses for Dolce & Gabbana, there was an assertive masculine profile about this offering.

"Chin up," she encouraged her first model as if this sentiment would somehow echo back to her. And then the audio began, "Who says women cannot, nay . . . should not rule the world?" Almost immediately, a retro version of the Kinks' gender-bending classic "Lola" could be heard throughout the room ("Well, girls will be boys, and boys will be girls. It's a mixed up, muddled up, shook up world, except for Lola.") Within two seconds, Sophia's first model pranced across the runway in her pinstripe suit, white shirt, power tie, and fedora. The next was a golfing outfit—replete with knickers, an argyle sweater, and an Irish golf hat. There were jeans and tan work shoes ensemble, plus a sheer see-through blouse for those who might need to be reminded that she had not "crossed over to the other side." And just for grins, there was a kilt shorter than usual, with 3" heels.

Sophia's fear? It might just be a bridge too far. Or worse yet, it would be compared to a knock off the Annie Hall era. It's impossible to not get sweaty palms with so much at stake. To this day, Sophia confesses she felt an invasion of butterflies. She also admits that this strange limbo of indecision was perhaps the most exciting moment of her life.

After the first five seconds, there was no response. Wait! Stop. Damn, there was tepid clapping. And then there was applause. Then there was more applause. And then there was that thunder that Sophia Senna had only dreamed about all her life.

To his credit, Domenico Dolce did visit her that night and shower her with accolades. He also offered to take financial responsibility for her fledgling design firm—with her name first and a subline that simply stated that this was a subsidiary of the Dolce & Gabbana Enterprise. If you have recently bought one of her Sophia Senna fedoras, you probably know that she gratefully declined.

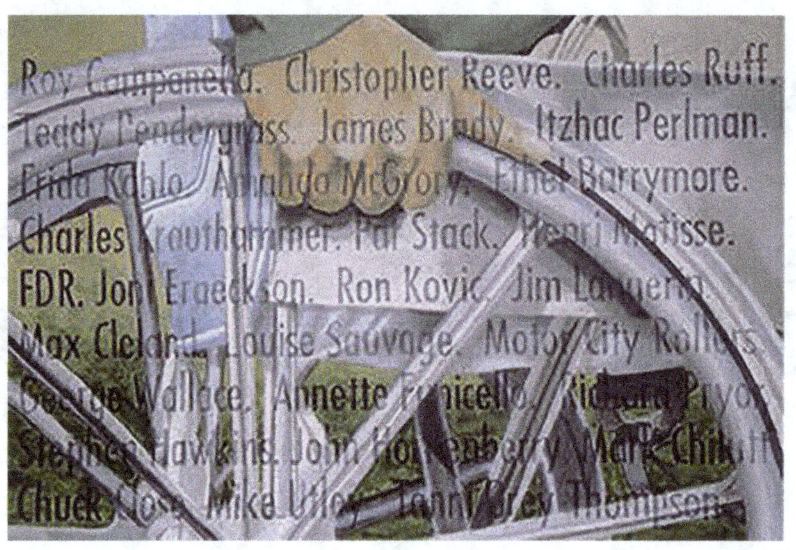

Wheels of Progress
Watercolor
30 × 24
2009

3.8 Seconds

Maurice Wallace has relived the event that forever changed his life hundreds of times. Like many of these tragedies, it seemed to happen in the blink of an eye. In fact, the entire sequence took about 3.8 seconds as the video camera captured with a ticking time line.

The place was called Angelo's Deli, and it had been a regular fixture of the north Philadelphia neighborhood for the past twenty years. It was always a tough working-class place, but it had lately become a tougher nonworking neighborhood, somewhat weirdly balanced by Temple University students who had sprawled into the area in search of affordable apartments.

At the time, Maurice was a third-year college student in psychology. As an African-American in an African-American neighborhood, he did not feel like a visual neon target for the thugs. As a matter of fact, he was a regular visitor to Angelo's Deli, where he would regularly get his toiletries, bread, microwavable dinners, and lottery tickets.

"Angelo, here's two bucks for a Mega Million ticket. I feel lucky today," he cheerfully told the middle-aged owner on the day it all happened. Before the deli owner could plug in the transaction, two teenage boys moved up to the counter to Maurice's right and pulled out a .38.

"Don't even think, old man," the one with the gun said. "Just hand over all your tens, twenties, and fifties."

After a weary sigh, the owner went to his cash register to take out his larger bills. Angelo had endured these incidents more than he would like to admit. He had learned it was easier and safer to surrender a few hundred dollars than
to fight.

At first, Maurice just stared at the two teenagers.

"What you lookin' at, sucker?" one thug snarled.

"You're doin' wrong," the young student said. "You wanna steal money from people who hang in to help this neighborhood?" At that point, Maurice, in a broad gesture, accidentally touched the gun, which touched off the temper of the robber, who whirled around and took a shot at Maurice Wallace. It happened to pierce his neck and his spinal cord, and crumble the young student. The bullies raced out of the deli. Everything was captured on videotape—all 3.8 seconds of the incident.

For several nights, the sequence was played on local Philadelphia TV stations. But after a few days, some new tragedy replaced it on the news cycle, and the perpetrators were never identified or caught.

At the time, Maurice was in the emergency ward with his distraught mother. Angelo visited several times, which kept the story alive for a few scant hours, but then it faded into the ether of competing news stories. Unfortunately, the results of the emergency surgery confirmed that Maurice would be a paraplegic for the rest of his life.

Rehab, counseling, church, various twelve-step programs—none of these measures changed the fact that Maurice Wallace will spend the next sixty years of his life pushing his own wheelchair.

Remarkably (for those of us who have never endured such a catastrophe), the young man persevered. With some financial assistance, he was able to return to Temple eighteen months later and gain his degree. On the heels of this, he went to law school and is now a rather celebrated defense attorney in Philadelphia. Like many law grads, he started in the prosecutor's office, but given his wit, drive, and legal skills, it was clear to many firms that the man could argue any case.

Sometimes, he finds himself defending perpetrators of gun violence. Not surprisingly, these are his most difficult cases. In this regard, his wheelchair and personal experience is ironically a plus. However, he still fears that he will someday have to defend the twosome who created his physical predicament. From a purely legal standpoint, he hopes he would never again recognize them. However, he knows that a 3.8-second review of the videotape might again make them immediately recognizable.

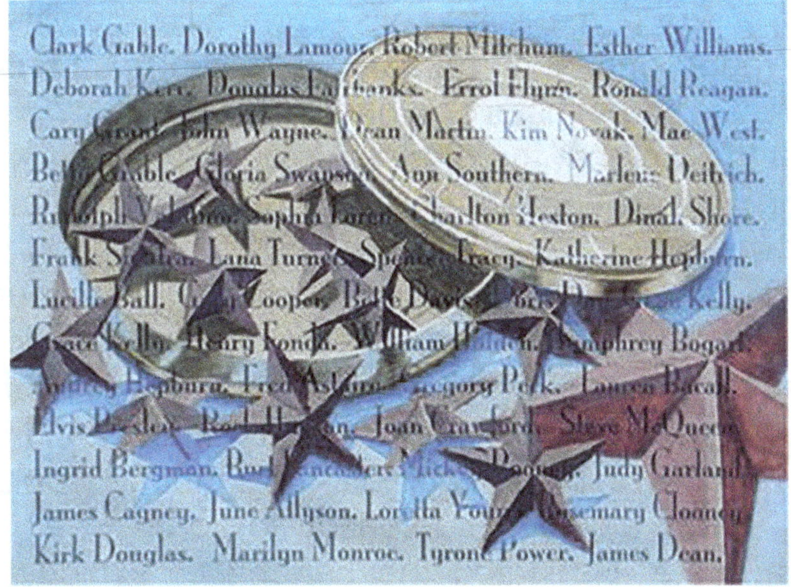

Old Stars
Watercolor
33 × 26
2008

Very Old Stars

Fittingly, the seventy-year-old movie theater on Fourth Street was called the Golden Standard. In its heyday in the mid-twentieth century, it premiered such classics as *Gone with the Wind*, *Sunset Boulevard*, and *Casablanca*. That was a long time ago. That was when the citizens of Louisville would dress up on dates to see the stars of the silver screen and lose themselves for a few hours in the celluloid magic of the movies.

As was common in many inner-city movie palaces, it became a rather threadbare showcase for black exploitation films in the early1980s. After a few years of dwindling audiences, this once-glittering cinema was shuttered.

That's when Bernard Harrison entered the picture. He had always been a fan of showbiz but was an even bigger fan of the real estate biz, especially when he could secure a sweet deal. This particular transaction was honey-dripping sugar.

According to his friends in government, he learned that the Golden Standard would soon be designated a historical landmark. As such, it provided rather generous dollars-and-cents advantages—the place qualified for a 20 percent tax offset on all rehabilitations, local property tax reductions, and charitable deductions on federal returns (since the theater had a history in the arts).

Add to that the fact that the thousands of young loft-loving college-educated Louisvillians wanted to reclaim the inner city for their urban lifestyle, and you have the perfect equation for a famous business.

Let's not race past that second last word in the previous sentence. While Mr. Harrison did not personally crave fame, he did appreciate that incandescent allure from Hollywood. Consequently, he chose to lionize those stars in his newly rehabbed Golden Standard Cinema. While he never promised the landmark folks that he would only show classic films, it was always his intention to do so. A big part of this was personal taste. He hated the car-chase, exploding-buildings, and CGI theory of moviemaking so prevalent today. A bigger part of his screenings had to do with an evangelical sense of mission. "If only people could rediscover these film classics and inspirational stars, the world would be a better place," he promised to the *Louisville Courier*, when the movie palace was again opened.

"If you build it, they will come," James Earl Jones announced in the mystical hit *Field of Dreams*. Unfortunately, reality and mysticism rarely meet. The people did not come to the black-and-white classic at the Golden Standard. In 2012, James Cagney, Dorothy Lamour, and Joan Crawford had little built-in box-office appeal.

An ordinary man might decide to pocket the profit and simply screen *Wedding Crashers 5*. Instead, Bernard Harrison somehow believed in the gestalt of the classic movie experience. Perhaps, he told his kids, it was time for him to be as creative as the studio chiefs. But how to do so and attract the weary workers of Louisville? For starters, he combined genres on each weekend—mafia movies, a Western weekend, a Bogart festival, a "Fall in love with Tracy and Hepburn" gala, an "Isn't Cary Grant Cool?" celebration. This started to attract an audience.

Then he added cuisine to the offering. Instead of gummy bears, whoppers, and Reese's pieces, he offered fettuccini Alfredo and calamari fritti for the mafia movies. The Western weekend featured pulled pork sandwiches. The "Cary Grant Cool" celebration was accompanied with ice-cream sandwiches, gelato, and flan. Local chefs began to compete for the star-studded evenings. As you might know from your own local community, this sort of integrated entertainment has become *de rigueur* among classic movie theaters.

Last June, Bernard Harrison passed away in peace at the age of eighty-two. At the time, the *Louisville Courier* did a two-column obit about his contribution to the community. This write-up thrilled his surviving sons and daughter. What thrilled them even more was the fact that today they just learned that, given his unique contribution to Hollywood legends, Bernard would be honored with a star on the Hollywood Walk of Fame next year. Quite appropriately, he will be forever seen between Mae West and Clark Gable.

If you're ever in the neighborhood, "Frankly, my dear, come up and see
him sometime."

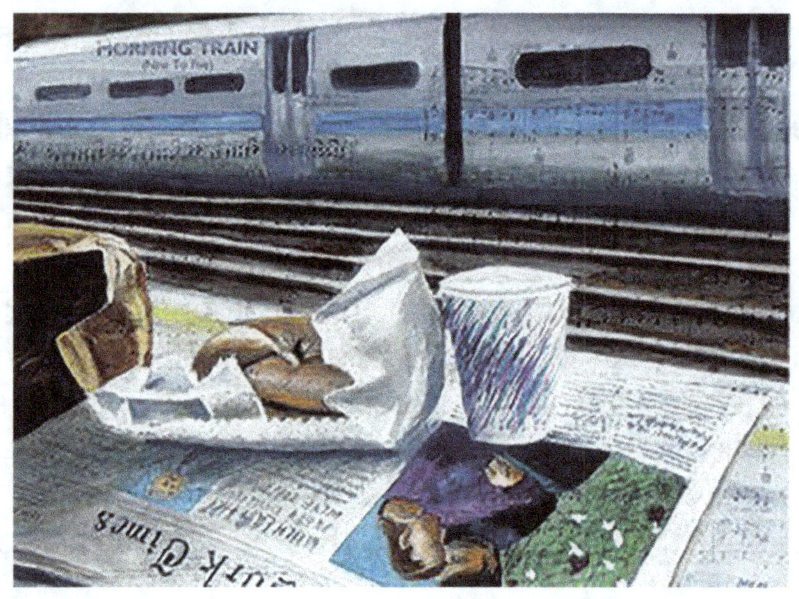

Morning Train
Pastel
30 × 24
2005

Morning Train

It had become a proud routine for fifty-five-year-old Bernie Cohen. He had taken the 7:50 a.m. express from Hastings to Grand Central every morning for the past thirty-two years. The day always started with a cream cheese bagel and the daily *New York Times.* Invariably, he and his friends boarded the third car and took the large facing seats by the door. Along the journey, they would discuss politics, sports, and family, even medical maladies. However, they rarely spoke of work.

That was a good thing since Bernie Cohen had been fired by the Barnes & Noble bookstore a month ago. Technically, it was a cutback since the big chain had decided to shutter one-third of their stores, including the one on Fourteenth Street. But it sure felt like a dismissal, especially since he was given packets of unemployment contacts and Cobra health-care forms.

He had told no one about this ugly turn of events—not his wife, not his grown-up kids, and certainly not his lifelong friends who shared that morning Metro–North train. It would be just too humiliating.

Worse still, it would deprive Bernie of the one remaining thing that made him feel like a valued team member.

He remembered when the fifth member of his group—a man named Ira Stein—lost his job ten years ago. Like most of his commuting cohorts, Bernie saw Ira a few times, but then the relationship withered with neglect. According to rumors, Ira had moved to the boondocks in central Pennsylvania, but nobody knew for sure since nobody spoke with unemployed Ira.

On this particular morning, Bernie enjoyed his morning regimen and boarded the 7:50 with a bounce in his step. Today would be different from the past two weeks. During that period, he had been rejected by every single bookshop in Manhattan. It was the same excuse from all the booksellers—declining volume due to the web and a struggle to even retain their own staff. To pass the days, he had visited a few art museums and taken a few bus and walking tours of New York City. It was already getting old.

Today, however, there was a flicker of hope. Bernie had contacted one of those recruiters given to him by the Barnes & Noble human resources staff, and they had actually called him back. The interview was set for 10:00 a.m., and Bernie was dressed in his best blue suit and striped tie for the event.

Alas, there was no job waiting for Bernie at this meeting. However, there was a frank discussion of his prospects and possible new avenues. Just about when it sounded hopeless, the interviewer admitted there was a possible position for a literary walking tour in lower Manhattan.

"I would love to do that," Bernie gushed. "How soon can they hire?"

"You can ask them in the interview next Wednesday. Meanwhile, I would brush up on Dorothy Parker, Truman Capote, F. Scott Fitzgerald, Saul Bellow, and anyone else you can think of."

"I've already studied them all," the former Barnes & Noble employee beamed.

As he boarded the 7:50 this Wednesday morning, he again hunkered down with his commuting buddies. He loved the camaraderie of this group and the daily repartee.

"Did you know that Arthur C. Clarke wrote *2001: A Space Odyssey* in the Chelsea Hotel?" Bernie buoyantly asked.

A few of his buddies looked up from their newspapers. One said, "Wow, someday you should do something with all that literary brainpower of yours. You know, like get on *Jeopardy* or teach or something."

Bernie shook his head. "Yeah, maybe I will someday," he said nonchalantly.

The interview was set for 11:00 a.m., and Bernie Cohen was bursting with literary factoids. If all went well, he would never have to admit that he had been fired. He would never have to endure the ignominy that befell Ira. He could remain part of the team. He could claim credit for redirecting his life and, perhaps, even become the envy of his stuck-in-the-same-job commuting friends.

"Maybe I'll do that someday," Bernie repeated and hoped so much that today could be that day.

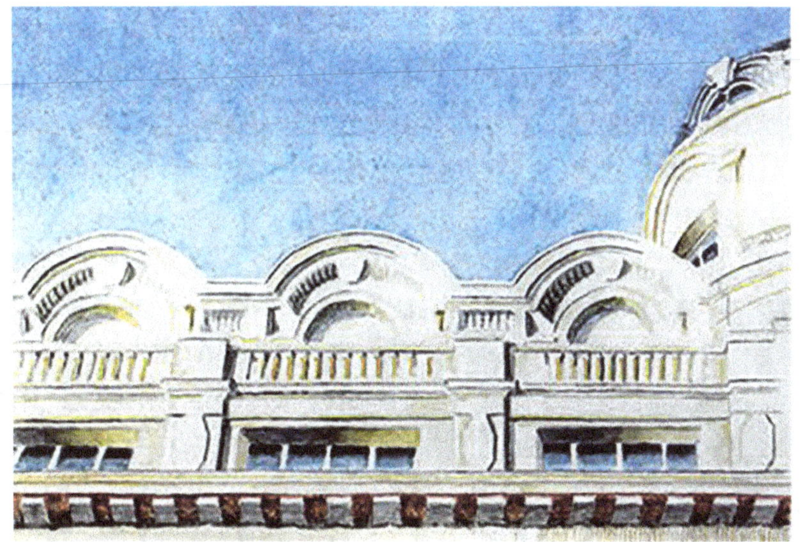

Two Blocks from the Louvre
Watercolor
27 × 20
2013

Two Blocks from the Louvre

Michelle Lepage always loved working in that landmark building on Rue de Louvre. The limestone structure was erected in 1872. It had grand wide windows and spacious offices. Most importantly, it was just two blocks from the world's most famous art museum.

That proximity was a boon for Michelle. At least once a week, she would spend her lunch hour inside the vast labyrinthine art space. Invariably, she would discover some insight and inspiration for the week ahead. At least that's the way it had gone for the past eight years.

During that time, she had been the arts and leisure reporter for *France* magazine. However, this was about to change. With many conflicting emotions, Michelle had tentatively agreed to take the plum position of CEO/editor-in-chief of *Paris Voice,* the more irreverent, upstart publication that had chased her for several years. It would mean more money, more publicity, more variety. It would come with a new roomy office in the Seventh Arrondissement, a long cab ride from the Louvre. Consequently, it would signify the end of her single-minded weekly passion with fine art.

The very thought of it increasingly depressed her.

"Bonjour, Mademoiselle Lepage," the Louvre guide smiled and motioned the woman to proceed through the turnstiles into centuries of art, sculpture, crafts, and artifacts. As usual, she took the escalator up toward the exhibits and instantly felt connected to a larger, more beautiful world.

At the same time, unbeknownst to Michelle, her coworkers were busy preparing a good-bye party for her. There was a cake, champagne, and a handwritten banner in the making.

Most members of the staff were frankly surprised that she had wanted this new position and career advancement. She had never struck them as overly ambitious. And then there was the easy, outgoing familiarity Michelle always exhibited with those in the office. The thirty-five-year-old single woman with no children seemed to regard her coworkers as family. As this was Michelle's last day at *France* magazine, many sad staffers remarked that it felt as if a dear sister was leaving home.

With a jumble of yin-yang emotions, Michelle proceeded to the Egyptian display in Salon 118. Unlike her usual dedicated focus, she could feel herself ambling from one room to the next in search of any insight that might inform her dilemma. The only thing that connected with her was a frieze in which all the figures stare in the same direction, left to right. At least in her current state of mind, it seemed to suggest that the expected outlook might be predictable but not exactly thrilling. Maybe that's what the artist meant. Maybe not. Maybe it was just her emotions telling her to rethink.

As she neared the Louvre exit, she took one remaining look at those caverns of artistic influence and wistfully headed back to her office. On this particular day, it seemed a shorter stroll than usual. However, it did afford her enough to time to wonder.

How could she possibly leave all this?

How could she possibly take a new job?

How could she possibly move to the swanky new offices in the Seventh Arrondissement?

Her coworkers were asking the same questions as they put the finishing touches on their handwritten banner.

As Michelle entered the elevator toward her floor, she wished the dilemma would go away. She wished the decision was over. She wished there would be some sign telling her what to do.

When the elevator doors opened, she saw it. In front of her were twenty coworkers, champagne glasses in hand, tacking up the banner that urged her to stay by simply stating, *"Rester."*

That afternoon, she called the people at *Paris Voice* and declined the offer.

"But why?" the shocked publisher asked.

"The people. The art. The heart. The place. I love this job. And besides, I'm just two blocks from the Louvre."

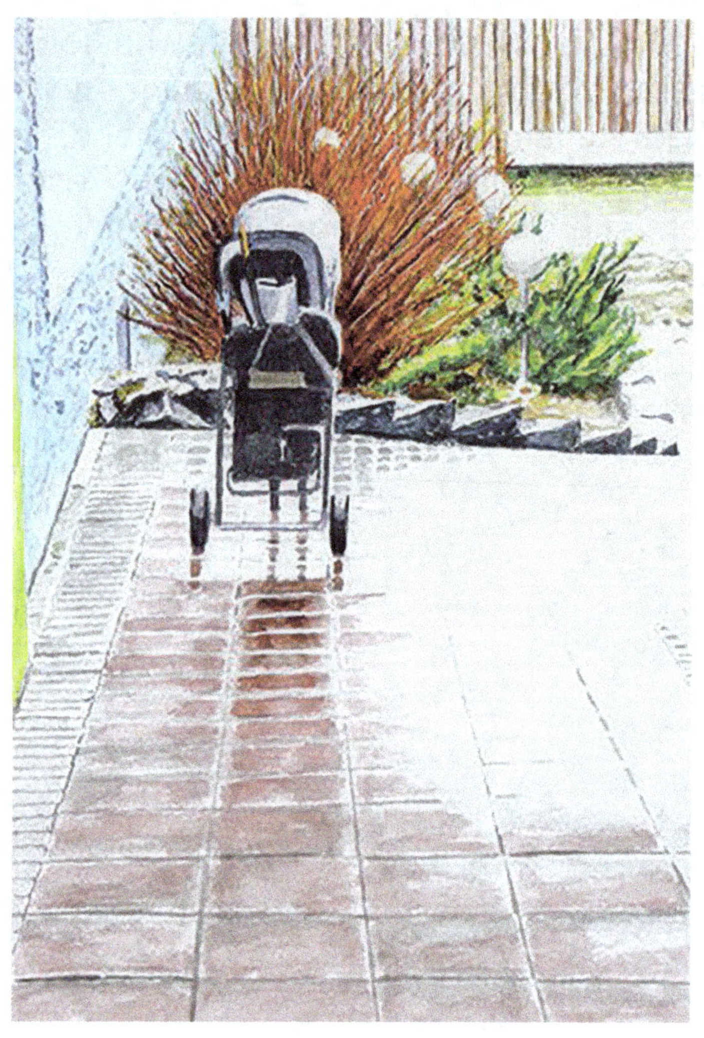

The Curious Baby Carriage

"It shouldn't be left out there in this horrid rain shower," eighty-six-year-old Mrs. Gladys Dalrymple said to her old friend as they walked along Park Street under their umbrellas. As everyone in the town of Bristol knew, the woman had a reputation for being the village busybody.

"Isn't that the Barkers' apartment?" Gladys asked, already knowing the answer.

"Yes, it is, and no, they don't have any kids," Maggie Dixon answered, anticipating the next question.

"Well, maybe they have some reckless guests who are visiting them. Maybe Americans. All I know is if their little one goes into that wet pram, he or she will surely be in danger of catching pneumonia. I really should tell them it's raining cats and dogs." With faux concern, the gossip queen headed toward the Barkers' door.

"Gladys, I think they know it's raining," Maggie grabbed her arm. "C'mon, I will buy you a tea." And with that, the two octogenarians headed to Pemberton's Café around the corner.

It was a ritual for the two women around 3:00 p.m. every day. The waitresses in the establishment knew that Gladys liked her Earl Grey with a chocolate-covered biscuit and that Maggie enjoyed hers with a raspberry jam scone.

This afternoon break was normally enough to soothe Gladys and quell her meddlesome chatter about the neighbors. A few months ago, such a tea break had taken her mind off old Charlie Hancock's supposed affair (the woman in question happened to be his younger sister). Years earlier, Gladys had also mistakenly accused the school principal of stealing a car (he actually bought the convertible). She also erroneously linked the local florist to a drug habit (the "pills" in question were only to keep her bouquets fresh). None of these muddled observations deterred her, but a soothing cup of tea could somehow calm her curiosity about the townspeople around her.

Maggie believed that this preoccupation with other people's personal business was a direct result of an unmarried, childless life. True, her own life had those same earmarks, but she was never nearly as nosy as her friend Gladys.

"More hot water?" the waitress asked the two ladies. Both smiled and rewarmed their teas. Just as Gladys took a small nibble of her chocolate-covered biscuit, the Barkers came into the café, accompanied by a young couple.

"Oh my god. I'll bet they left their baby at home . . . all alone," Gladys whispered to her friend.

"Gladys, relax."

Instead, the busybody sashayed over to Mr. and Mrs. Barker and introduced herself to the visitors. Unlike the old woman's fantasy, the couple was not from the United States. In fact, they weren't even a couple. Both were work associates of Mr. Barker—one from London, one from Brighton. And contrary to her imagination, they did not have a young baby.

"But what about the rain-drenched pram?" Gladys skeptically asked.

"Oh, that's mine," Mrs. Barker laughed. "I just got that at a garage sale! It costs me next to nothing."

"But, you don't have a little—" Mrs. Dalrymple said.

"No, but I have a garden outside in that courtyard. And I needed something to carry my tools and transport the pansies, geraniums, and impatiens. It's a little wobbly, but it does the trick."

"Hmmm," Gladys responded dubiously. She then forced a smile and said her good-byes.

The two elderly women silently left Pemberton's and started the five-block walk back to their neighborhood. The aftermath of the rain had left a fragrant smell, but there was still tension in the air. Finally, Maggie broke the ice. "You have to quit imagining the worst of people."

"Hmmm," Gladys answered and then stopped and stared at that lonely pram in the Barkers' courtyard. "I wonder why she couldn't find a wheelbarrow at the garage sale." She then ambled over to the carriage to inspect the inside. No dirt. No tools. No plant containers.

"Curious, don't you think?" Gladys said.

"No. Not really," her best friend answered.

"I wonder if she's trying to get pregnant," Gladys posited.

"Stop it."

"Maybe she can't. Maybe Mr. Barker can only shoot blanks."

"Gladys!"

And so it went for the remainder of their short journey to their neighborhood, and it would continue until 3:00 p.m. the next day until the Earl Grey tea could once again suppress the wicked imagination of Gladys Dalrymple.

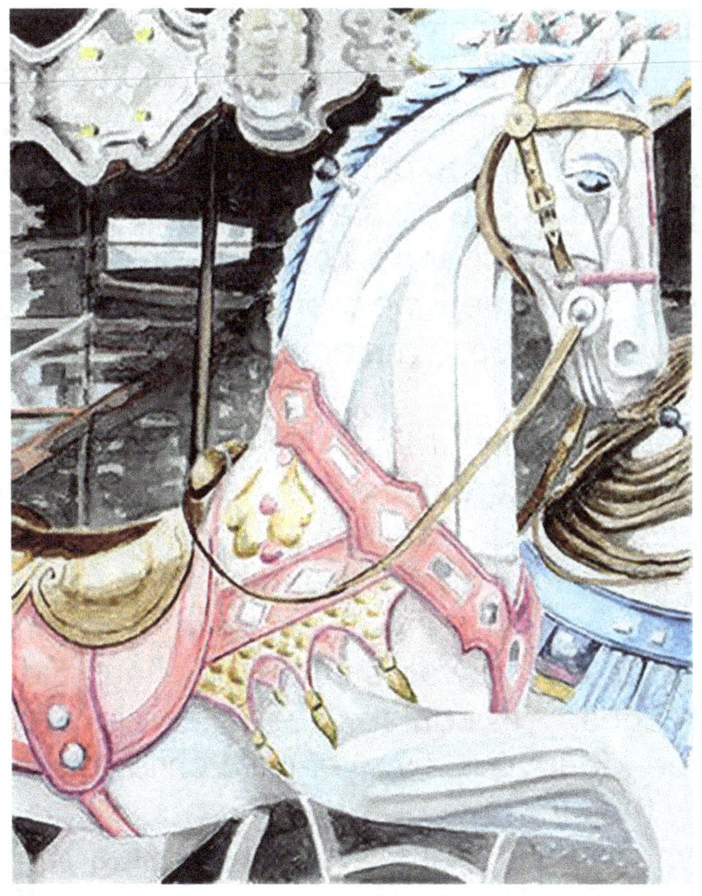

Carousel

For the past thirty-seven years, the Carousel du Cheveax had been a labor of love for Manny Morales. Every morning, before Rye Playland opened at 9:00 a.m., Morales would spend forty-five minutes giving each horse a soapy sponge bath of warm water and Fabuloso cleaning fluid. He would then give the vintage 1912 attraction a ten-minute test run to make sure there were no creaks, squeaks, or grinding sounds from the machinery. Lastly, he would test the volume, timber, and balance of the prerecorded glockenspiel and accordion music that accompanied the excursion, as Morales liked the call it.

He always preferred that term to the more popular, mundane description: a ride. It implied that the circular journey was a journey into history, grandeur, and chivalrous adventure.

Unfortunately, few visitors to the park shared that romantic fantasy these days. With increasing regularity, they seemed to prefer the more violent, gut-wrenching experiences. The Mad Rat, for example, jarred passengers around corners at forty miles per hour and evoked screams. Twenty yards farther away, Sampson's Squeeze used 2 g's of centrifugal force to frighten the teenage crowds. The latest darling of the park, the Devil's Drop, simulated a suicidal three-story jump off a building.

As the most senior engineer, Morales had been given the option of maintaining these new attractions but had always opted to be the guardian of the Carousel du Cheveax.

He liked the fact that it was still the hub of the entire park—with all the more gruesome experiences sprawling out from its central location. In that respect, it was still the meeting and focal point for families of all ages. Of course, the clientele was now mostly restricted to three-, four-, and five-year-old children who were usually accompanied by their parents or grandparents.

Consequently, it was somewhat surprising when a dozen teenagers lined up for this late-evening excursion. Over the years, Morales had learned to be wary of this group on these horses. A few years back, several hooligans had tried to spray-paint graffiti on the antique steeds. In fact, they even had their graffiti weapons drawn when Morales affected a sudden stop and toppled the boys off the horses. Mortified with the spill and alarmed at the siren, the boys scurried away with no harm done.

Tonight, Morales had his finger on that same panic button as he carefully watched the teenagers. He glanced at the video cameras that were creating a nonstop record of the potential troublemakers. He then looked at his wristwatch and marked 8:42 p.m., just in case a scuffle ensued and authorities would need some shorthand of the time things got out of hand.

After the customary four-minute journey, Manny slowed the horses to a crawl and dialed down the volume of the music as an encouragement to exit. However, the ruffians did not budge.

"One more go-around, old man," one of the boys called out.

"Gotta make room for other people," the operator answered.

"There aren't any other people."

"But it's nearly closing time," Manny sighed.

"No! Run the damn thing again, old man," the same kid commanded.

Morales looked back at the gang and counted six of them. Six against one—not a fair fight.

He then took a deep breath and trudged back to his small operating station. As he did so, he found three dads with their young kids waiting in line.

"I want to go too," another four-year-old called out in the distance and raced up to the line with his dad. Soon, three other pairs joined them. One by one, they raced around the circle, looking for their own particular favorite horse and precariously settled into place with the help of a parent.

Morales looked back at his group of passengers and then asked "Everyone ready?"

"Wait!" the lead teenager called out and motioned for the rest of his posse to dismount. "Maybe some other time, old man," he grumbled and exited by the loading station. As he did so, he reached into his pocket and took out a spray can and jetted some fresh paint on Morales's tennis shoes. Immediately, the group of teenagers rudely guffawed and sprinted away.

Manny Morales stood motionless for a moment while his frustration morphed into a trifecta of happiness. It pleased him that his antennae correctly assessed the inherent danger of the gang. He was relieved that it only resulted in a graffiti smudge on his well-worn shoes. But most of all, he was tickled that the carousel was now filled, as it should be, with wide-eyed young kids and their parents.

"Everyone hold on tight," he advised. He then pushed the lever to slowly start the horses and proudly smiled at the eternally bonding excursion.

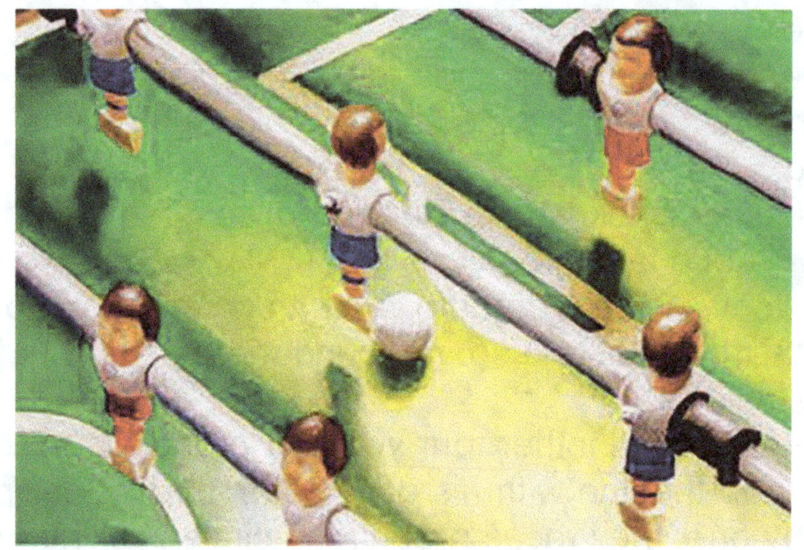

He Shoots!
He Scores . . . Maybe

In their quieter moments, both men admitted it was just idiotic to continue this competitive rivalry thirty years after college.

However, James Wellborn and Mickey "Spider" Markley could never resist. They had always been friendly foes since their first tryout on the Indiana University football team. At the time, both eighteen-year-olds had been given scholarships, and both were expected to make the team. However, there was only one starting defensive safety slot, and Spider got it.

James, on the other hand, became the star wide receiver in his sophomore year and got the coed that Mickey had first spotted, at least for a season.

In their senior year, both were tenth-round NFL draft picks—Spider with the Philadelphia Eagles, James with the Chicago Bears. Neither one made the cut; however, James did enjoy mini bragging rights since he lasted in the pro camp four full days longer than Mickey.

"It doesn't matter! Neither one of us made the damn teams," Spider often reminded his friend.

"Well, I did stay on my team longer. That's just a fact. Maybe it's too painful for you to admit, but hey, it happened," James said with a sly smile and a wink toward his friend.

"Just center the ball, dammit," Spider shook his head and invited his friend to drop the foosball on the centerline. It was a game they had picked up at Northwestern, where they both attended business school. They would often play grudge matches late into the night, with relatively even scores.

Their rivalry continued after graduation. James landed a plush job at CBS. Spider, who now preferred to be called Michael C. Markley, landed a similar marketing position at NBC. The ratings battle between the two networks just intensified their competitive juices. When NBC had the ratings edge, James just loved to rub it in. When CBS took the lead briefly, Spider sent his friend complimentary DVDs of the top-rated shows.

"That was a ridiculously lucky ricochet!" James shouted when the foosball caromed off the corner, hit the immobile defender in blue, and squibbed into the goal.

"I planned it that way." Spider shrugged.

"Bullshit," James protested. "Go again," he said and dropped the foosball in the center of the table.

This back-and-forth, ebb and flow again held sway.

Bear in mind, there had always been a few brief periods of noncombative peace in the men's relationships. For example, they were both best men at each other's weddings (although they did try to outdo each other with competing toasts). However, when Spider had the first son, he strutted like a peacock for two months until James's son, Blake, evened that playing field.

At this ironic moment, fifteen-year-old Blake Markley entered the family room and flipped on the TV. When the boy innocently entered the room, James fired a foosball bullet that was intercepted by Spider's lightning-fast goalie defense.

"It crossed the goal line," James hooted and performed a victory dance.

"I stopped it before it completely crossed the line," Spider howled with every ounce of sincerity.

"It's a fucking winning goal!" James screamed.

"It was not," Spider belted and then turned to his son. "Blake, you were walking into the room when my courageous save was made. Did you see the miraculous block?"

Blake interrupted his MTV viewing to view the two grown men. The kid then wearily buried his head for a second before trudging out of the room. "I'm going upstairs," he sighed. "I say you two maniacs play a tiebreaker."

James and Spider silently watched the kid walk up the stairs to his wired TV set. The two men looked at each other. They sighed. They smiled. And then they laughed aloud. After five minutes of this goofy, gleeful equilibrium, Spider picked up the foosball and held it head-high above the table.

"James, the score in games is 23–23. Should we play the next game as winner takes all?"

Without answering, the foosball was suddenly in play. With an amazing flip from Spider's forward line, the score was suddenly 1–0. At the conclusion of that goal, James answered his question. "No! Absolutely not! Winner must win by two!"

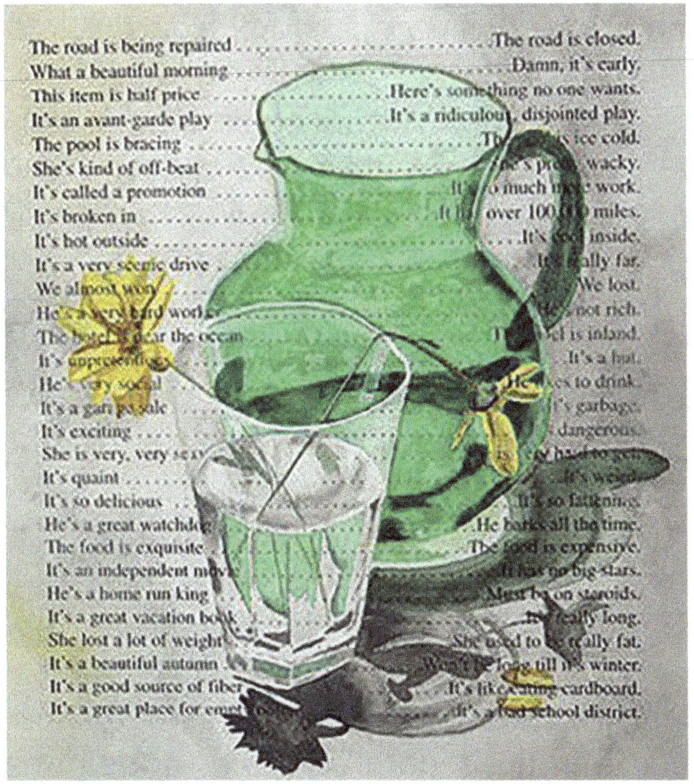

The Glass Is . . .
Watercolor
24 × 28
2006

The Glass Is . . .

Eva Dougherty poured the Stoli up to the midpoint in her tumbler and flashed upon the words that her mother used to tell her as a grade-schooler: "Don't be such a pessimist. All you ever see is the glass half empty. Eva dear, if you think positive thoughts, good things can happen for you."

For Eva, now twenty-nine, that had rarely been the case. Always chubby, she had never found true love. On the other hand, she had enjoyed some measure of success in the workplace. After graduating from Temple University with a degree in communication, the woman had logged long hours at a Philadelphia PR firm. To be honest, she never found it thrilling, but she always thought she was highly regarded until this afternoon. Everyone in the office knew that cutbacks were coming, but for Eva, it came as a surprise, especially in view of all the fake positive energy she threw into each grueling day.

As she sipped her vodka, she couldn't help but think that her mother had been wrong about all that optimism stuff. After all, the woman had lived a saintly life as a Catholic charities worker and then got struck with ovarian cancer. "How fair is that?" Eva remembered asking her mom in her closing days. She had reached for her daughter's hand and said, "Eva dear, it has nothing to do with fair. It has everything to do with believing that there's something better around the corner." Her mother then took a sip from her hospital cup. "And I do."

Eva wished she did. But as she looked around her lonely one-bedroom apartment, she knew she did not.

Another sip. By now, it was much less than half full. Just then, her landline rang. She looked on the ID and saw that it was a call from Bill Bernstein, one of her coworkers at the PR shop. The roly-poly print director had been fired just before her appointment to enter the corner office and hear the fateful news.

"Eva Dougherty? What are you doing?"

After a few seconds, she answered, "Nothing."

"Well, a bunch of us are down at the Happy Rooster on Rittenhouse Square. Hey, eight of us got the ax today. Thought I'd give you a call to join the joyous wake. You should come since we're all in the same boat."

"Oh, I don't know," Eva, said. "I don't know," she repeated louder as she tried to be heard over the background din of the bar. Fact is, she rarely socialized with any of her coworkers, and this was definitely a call out of nowhere. Perhaps the gallows humor of the day had prompted the invitation. "Hey, Eva. C'mon. The agency was a shit hole. Agree?"

"Yes, it was," Eva responded, for the first time using the past tense of employment.

"We all hated coming in every day. Right?"

"This is true."

"So we're all here together to plot our next assault on fame and fortune. You should join us."

A pause. For a brief second, Eva thought she was hearing a voice from her childhood.

"Hey, this might end up being the best thing that ever happened to all of us," Bill Bernstein added.

After a few seconds, Eva answered, "Why not?" She grabbed her coat and looked forward to raising another glass with her newfound support group. Hell, she might even begin to believe that glass could be half-full. As she waved for a cab, she smiled and couldn't help but think her mom might be proud of her.

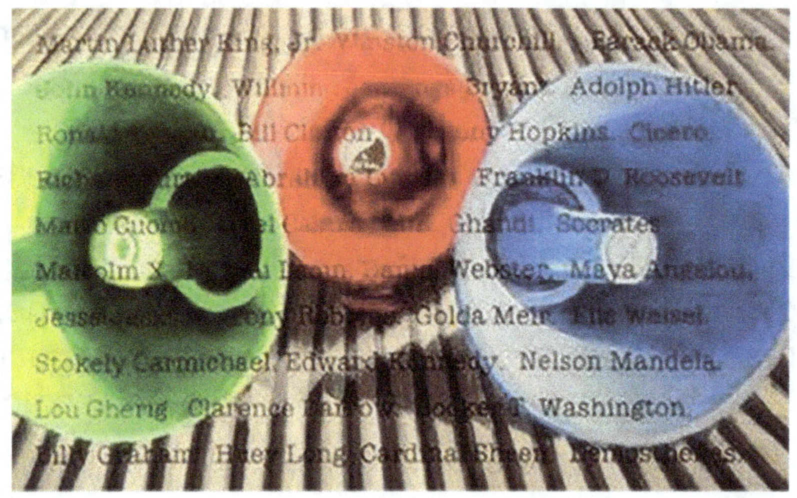

Colorful Speakers
Pastel
30 × 22
2009

Colorful Speakers

There are thousands of eager actors who descend upon Broadway every year, after being urged by the citizens of Springfield, Greenville, and Franklin, Anystate, USA, as the most amazing orators ever to be heard. As is most often the case, it's a flattering exaggeration. True, these hopefuls may have done a memorable job in the high school musical or the valedictorian's address, but they will never be in the league of Martin Luther King, JFK, Ronald Reagan, or even Richard Burton.

However, eight-year-old Kordell Washington had never heard of any of these luminaries and was consequently unaware of any preconceived comparisons. That was probably a good thing since it allowed the young boy to address the congregation at the Andrews Baptist Church in North Carolina freely, instinctively, and spontaneously.

The kid was undeterred by age. "Do you see heaven?" he asked in a roller-coaster voice an eighty-year-old woman on this particular morning. Without waiting for a response, the young evangelist answered. "I do. And it's beee-uuu-tiful! You're gonna love it when the time comes!" On cue, the crowd applauded, the organist began playing "Closer My God to Thee." At the same time, Mitch Morgan, the local stringer for *Time* magazine, was taking notes.

After the service, the writer waited for the young boy and asked for a few minutes outside the church door. "Do you write it out ahead of time?" Morgan asked. "It just comes to me." Kordell shrugged, and by then, his mom and dad joined him and skeptically asked what "this interview" was all about.

"I've heard of his speaking skills all the way to Asheville," the reporter answered. "If I could spend thirty minutes with him, in your presence of course, I might be able to make him and the church more famous . . . and more heavily attended." Mitchell Morgan knew the territory. He knew how to appeal to local evangelicals. He understood that ego alone was not enough for the Baptist crown. Above all, he knew how to get a story.

In the next thirty minutes, he sat down with young Kordell, his mom, and his dad in the local coffee shop. As the young boy spoke, the reporter scribbled pages of notes and then took a few pictures in front of the church. Some were with the parents. The most promising one was with the kid alone, with his arms outstretched and reaching up to the heavens.

The 1974 *Time* magazine article titled "The Boy Has a Gift" catapulted Kordell as one of the most celebrated evangelists in the country. Within nine years, the teenager had guest spots on Sunday morning religious broadcasts. Within the next decade, he had his own regular (and profitable) telecast. His overall message was "God is everywhere . . . every day if we allow him." Yes, it had political overtones about caring for our brethren. Within the next four years, he was featured on *Meet the Press* and *Face the Nation.*

Ironically, his reputation as "the most colorful young speaker in America" backfired in 2004. Kordell was scheduled at the Democratic Convention on day 2. He was touted as the man who might unlock the greed of the '90s and encourage the liberal base to respond to the growing needs of poverty in America.

This was just a matter of bad timing.

You see, there was this other African-American speaker from Illinois who was scheduled to deliver the keynote address on day 1. The young state senator talked about a melding of interests from people of all political stripes, religious faiths, and socioeconomic strata. His most famous line was "There is no red America. Or Blue America. There is only one United States of America."

The man's name was Barack Hussein Obama.

At the time, few knew him. But after Mitch Morgan's cover story in *Time* magazine, the man became a household word. At 2:00 a.m. on day 2, a few people said a few nice things about a young evangelist called Kordell Washington, who delivered his address after midnight. Thanks to the help of Mr. Obama, the rousing orator is now the pastor of the Trinity United Church of Christ, replacing the problematic chief called Rev. Jeremiah Wright.

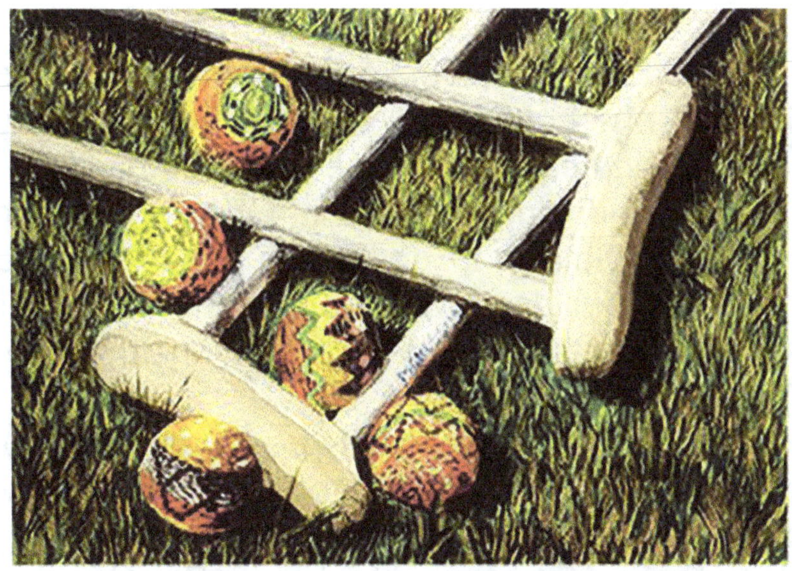

Hobbled Hacky Sack
Watercolor
22 × 17
2013

The Hobbled Hacky Sacker

It had been a long time since I stood outside the circle of Hacky Sackers and craved an invitation to join the group. Of all things, a bullshit injury serendipitously put me there.

As a professional athlete, I always hated it when the team physician's prognosis sidelined me. I understand that it's an occupational hazard. The philosophy goes like this: better off nursing your little owie over several days, rather than reinjure it or, worse yet, aggravate the injury, which can result in a lawsuit under the heading of organizational negligence.

However, as someone who has played soccer for fourteen years, including my most recent stint as eight-year professional for the LA Galaxy, I believe I know something about the personal limitations of a bad ankle sprain. Generally, I believe one should tape it up and then walk on it until it doesn't hurt. Ultimately, I believe that if you can run and kick with it, you play. Period. It's soccer, after all (or fútbol, as we call it in Europe). It's not patty-cake.

After my owie on Friday, the team doctor advised Coach Bruce Arena that I should rest the right leg, 100 percent. Bear in mind, there was no torn ligament, no stress fracture, just an ankle sprain.

But since it was my third one in a month, the verdict was that I should exert "no load whatsoever" on my right leg. Despite the fact that I only "injured" one right ankle, they gave me two crutches (so I didn't favor one leg and cause damage to the other). Damn, this anal microcarefulness was driving me batshit. Oh yeah, one more thing, I was advised by the Galaxy to go to the beach and keep the leg elevated for at least four days. "We don't want to hear an argument from you," Coach Arena decreed. "It's for your own good and the good of the team."

I chose to go to Venice Beach, partly because I love the homeless dogs on the sidewalks, partly because I correctly believed I would not find a claque of reporters and soccer fans trailing me, as they would in Malibu, Santa Monica, or Manhattan Beach.

Other than the medicinal drug dealers, what I did find were weightlifters (Arnold used to work out there), svelte beach volleyballers, and circles of teenagers kicking those colorful Hacky Sack balls in the air. For the most part, they are Latinos—from Peru, Argentina, and Brazil. Given the locale, there are plenty of Mexican Hacky Sackers too. But they do not have the finesse of the lower-South Americans.

What I most love about this sport is that it is pointless. There is no score. There are no winners or losers. It's more like a Latino version of catch—a sort of communal give-and-take that requires skill but no competitive arithmetic. In that respect, it is pure athleticism.

As a teenager, I used to kick for hours on the beaches of Ipanema. Despite the fact that I am now twelve years past that era, I desperately wanted to join the circle. The various teenagers eyed me like a geezer, especially since I was walking on crutches. As a not-so-subtle solicitation, I dropped my two crutches on their assortment of balls and limped closer to the group.

Finally, Miguel, the dark Hispanic leader of the troupe, looked my way and gestured in a manner that could clearly be interpreted as "What's up with you, Mr. Grown-Up Man?" I chose to interpret it another way: "Do you care to join us?" With a few winces, I joined the group and kept the small ball alive. For the most part, I balanced my body on my good left foot and kicked with some pain from my heavily taped right—sometimes multiple times in the air, sometimes to applause, sometimes just to keep the ball moving, and always to feel part of the ragtag team.

After an hour of Hacky Sack acrobatics, we all walked away, and Miguel asked, "Mañana, a la siempre hora?"

I proudly grabbed my crutches and answered, "Sí!"

For the next four hours, I elevated my right ankle as promised.

For the next four days, I anonymously played Hacky Sack with my younger compadres at Venice Beach and did some elevation in the afternoon.

Today, I spoke with the team physician. Since the Galaxy does not have a game in the next two days, I told him that perhaps I needed one more day to heal the right ankle.

It was a beautiful Hacky Sack game this afternoon. I no longer have a limp, nor have any need to favor my right ankle. I am reminded how much I love the beauty of teamwork. I will be a better Galaxy player tomorrow. But today, I am in heaven with those anonymous strangers who love the artistry of the feet.

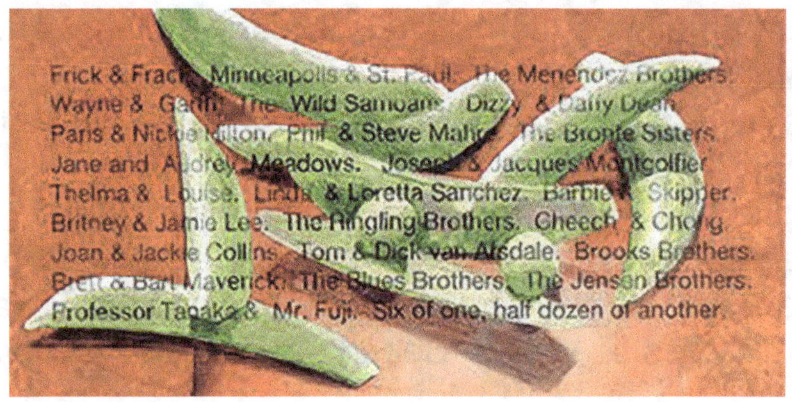

Two Peas in a Pod
Watercolor
30 × 20
2009

Two Peas in a Pod

Even in the third grade, many people thought Linda Flynn and Lauren Turner were twins, or at least cousins. The fact that they both had red hair and wore the identical blue plaid uniforms of Our Lady of Victory Elementary School gave this mirrored impression to casual observers.

However, their similarities were more than physical. They both preferred reading and writing to arithmetic. They both played soccer —Linda the left wing, Lauren the right wing. They had the same taste in music and in movies, and they rarely disagreed on their opinionated reviews. In the summer, when the normal school bonds become more elastic, the two girls insisted on going to the same summer sleepaway camps. As teenage girls, they both matured at about the same time, so the sex-hungry young boys in their class diminished any disparity in their development.

Even the great divide of most young adults—college—was minimized. They both applied to seven or eight universities, and at least five of these were the same schools. However, there were caution flags: Mr. and Mrs. Flynn did suggest that perhaps it was time for Linda to "stand on her own two feet." Actually, Ms. Turner had the same instinct and gently advised her daughter to "perhaps pursue her own path." Both girls ended up at the Johnson & Wales

Culinary School in Providence, Rhode Island, and all Manhattan parents had a gourmet celebration brunch together.

Even for graduates of one of the nation's best cooking schools, the culinary world is not an easy road. The hours are long, the work is sweaty, and the pressure is intense. At service time, there are not many giggles on the line. On the other hand, there is an amazing camaraderie in the kitchen, especially among those who learn to cover each other's backsides when they inevitably get caught "in the weeds."

Given the adrenaline released every night, the typical custom, especially among young cooks, is to gather for a late-night drink or two and perhaps some

3:00 a.m. scrambled eggs, just as a way to slowly decompress. For Linda, that hangout was Blue Ribbon Café in Soho. For Lauren and her kitchen crew, it was normally the Empire Diner.

And so finally, the two peas in a pod had somewhat separate orbs.

The divergence saddened both young women. After fourteen months of dedicated self-styled success, they decided to join forces and open La Souperie in the Flatiron District of New York. It was a rather remarkable success, and the two stunning redheads were lionized in a recent restaurant review in *New York Magazine.* "Equally attractive, the two *chefs extraordinaire* make magic in every dish, and with every customer."

Enticed, two reviewers for Zagat's—one is called Matt, the other Mitchell—decided to make an unannounced visit to the place and sample the menu.

"Are you twins?" the waitress innocently asked the two diners.

"No, but we are hungry," Matt answered.

"I was going to say the same thing," Mitchell dittoed.

When the bowls were served with fresh French baguettes, Linda visited the duo to ask if the food and service lived up to expectations. Five minutes later, the two chefs switched stations, and Lauren visited the same table with the temptation to sample a little dessert. Two crème brûlées and two espressos later, the young men were raving. To complete the après-hours satisfaction, the two M-and-M twins and the two L-and-L twins ended up in the same apartment.

Fast forward: six months. To put it mildly, it has been an interesting relationship. True, all parties love food. True, both the male and female counterparts bear some resemblance to each other. In retrospect, this confusion has proved vexing and exciting to all parties. Yes, we are taught to live as complete, unique individuals. On the other hand, the opportunity to vicariously live a barely alternative life with a barely alternative sexual partner is also quite appealing.

Linda?

Lauren?

Matt?

Mitchell?

Who's who? And what is your appetite tonight?

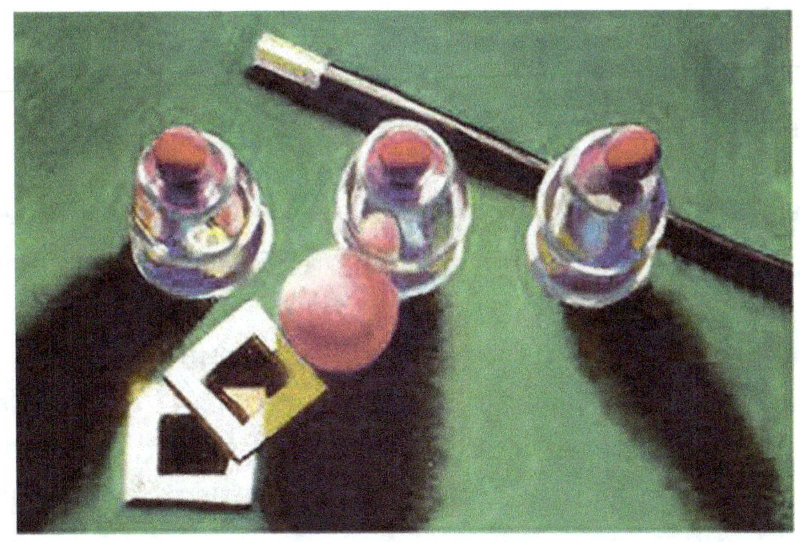

Cups and Balls
Pastel
24 × 18
2002

Marco's Secret Cup-and-Ball Routine

On June 18, 2011, Marco d'Marvel performed his last cup-and-ball routine. The man's particular handling was legendary among professional magicians and quite a secret in both magic societies—namely, SAM and the IBM.

First, allow me to explain the effect. After making small balls multiply and vanish under the three silver cups, Marco added a unique twist. He would spread a deck of cards and then ask two participants to freely make selections.Drumroll. Patter. Time for his finale. Under the center cup, he would reveal a large ball. Under the other two, he would reveal photo slides that would miraculously match the two cards held by his "marks."

Most people would say, "Holy shit." One profane gentleman said, "Holy fucking shit!" One man actually shit in his pants. The ta-da finish had that kind of impact.

For years, fellow magicians urged Marco to share his secret. Unlike most professionals who willingly will sell their tricks to other magicians on a CD for $20–$30, Marco always resisted this temptation since this particular effect was his stock and trade and, as a result, his claim to fame.

Unfortunately, that fame was about to come to an end. On June 19, after the show, Marco d'Marvel felt what he thought was a muscle ache up and down his right arm. He soon began to feel dizzy. Then his speech began to slur. After a half hour of feeling so off-kilter, he finally went to the hospital.

The stroke he suffered was not life threatening. It did not result in total paralysis or epilepsy. However, the aftereffects were devastating for a magician like Marco. His usual clever repartee was now halting. Worse yet, the required dexterity of his right hand was now forever absent.

Consequently, Marco d'Marvel went into a deep depression. At the age of sixty-four, he had figured he had a good ten more years ahead of him. After all, sometime in their midseventies, lots of magicians get the shakes or lose legerdemain or just want to go play shuffleboard in the Florida sun. That he could accept. But at sixty-four, the inability to perform magic was a crushing premature blow. Besides, what else could he do? He instinctively believed he was just too old to start something brand-new and too young for shuffleboard.

Occasionally, his magic friends would call and take him to lunch. Often, they would share a new trick or two with him. Ironically, it did not cheer him up since in his condition, there was little he could share with them.

This week, one of those friends—a man named Gene DeVoto—invited him for a cup of coffee and then made a proposition to Marco. "You know, I have this city's biggest magic shop," Gene said. "This week, two of my young assistants got cruise-ship gigs, so I'm very shorthanded. I could really use your expertise in the shop, behind the counter."

Marco had never seen himself as a clerk. On the other hand, it was an opportunity to at least surround himself with the world of magic. He sat silent for a few minutes and thought about the pros and cons, and then his eyes welled with tears. "Gene, I appreciate the overture," Marco struggled to explain, "but I can't even demonstrate the easiest trick. My right hand doesn't work."

"I already thought about that," Gene responded. "But your reputation and recommendation is enough to sell any trick. Besides, if someone wants a tease of how it might be presented, one of the young bucks can do that for you."

That was four years ago. Most of the time, Marco d'Marvel is the main attraction and a very persuasive hit with buying customers. Most days, it feels like heaven to expose interested souls to the possibilities of magic. When the occasional client asks to see the effect, he motions for young Tony to demo the miracle but never the secret. "You gotta buy that," Marco usually says, "and you will after big Tony shows you the presentation. Otherwise, he gets mad. And you don't want to see big Tony mad." It usually gets a laugh. It almost always sells the trick.

Last week, Marco did something he thought he would never do. He agreed to create a CD showcasing his most famous propriety cup-and-ball routine. *It's stupid and selfish to keep the joy of this effect all to myself*, he finally reasoned. His favorite demo man, Big Tony, performs the miracle and later explains the technique. It is now the largest selling CD in Gene DeVoto's magic shop and in many shops around the country.

Incidentally, if you look closely at the presentation, you will see a man who selects one of the cards and is so amazed that a photo slide of his selection is revealed under a cup he utters a stroke-accented "holy shit." It was a reaction Marco d'Marvel had learned from performing the miracle hundreds of times, and it was a happy response to the fact that he could somehow still play a role in the magical world.

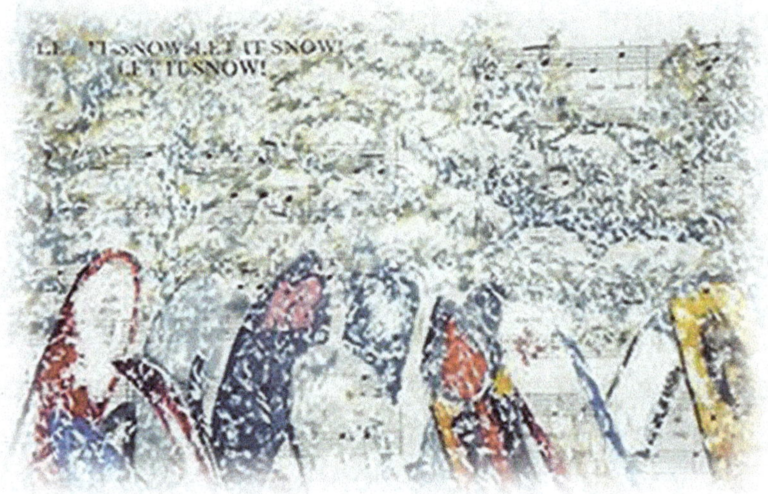

Let It Snow. Let It Snow. Let It Snow.
Pastel
30 × 24
2003

Let It Snow. Let It Snow. Let It Snow.

Ronald Bernstein had been planning on this trip to Jackson Hole for the past three years. Last January, he had to cancel for an important business meeting. The year before, his mother was taken ill and felt it best to stay with her in the Boston area. This year, he had cleared the decks at work and had even bought new parabolic skis. He had his airline ticket, hotel reservations, and rental car all ready to go. Hey, he even made arrangements to have the liquor cabinet prestocked! His West Coast friends, who had flown out a day earlier, had promised to supply the condo rental with plenty of beer, wine, and tequila. "All we need now is some fresh powder," he said aloud to the stranger in seat 18B, who just grunted and returned to reading his magazine.

Indeed, a new blanket of virgin white would be nice. It had been an unusually dry Thanksgiving and Christmas in the Tetons, but modern snowmaking made the mountain skiable, though not ideal. However, Ronald knew these conditions were an anomaly. Given the fact that Jackson Hole was at the upper reaches of the Rockies, a generous dump of snow could happen on any given day.

Today would be more than generous. As a matter of fact, it was a downright whiteout with a nonstop accumulation of sixteen fresh inches and a sudden temperature drop to twenty degrees, which made the entire area a nonstop ice rink. Consequently, all the roads were closed by noon. By 3:00 p.m., all the state airports were closed.

"Ladies and Gentlemen, we've got some very difficult, challenging conditions outside, so we recommend you keep your seat belts fastened," the pilot announced in his most reassuring movieland voice. "And in the interest of safety, perhaps with an abundance of caution, we are going to have to divert our landing away from Jackson Hole, which is in the midst of dangerous blizzard. Instead, we will be landing at McCarran International Airport in Las Vegas. There will be ground personnel available to help with your connections or passenger needs."

There was a collective groan from the 335 passengers, but none louder than the wail of Ronald Bernstein. The passenger in 18B stopped reading his magazine and shrugged at the disappointed skier. "It's probably for the best," he volunteered, as if that sage advice would somehow help.

Upon landing, Bernstein called his friends in Jackson Hole, who reassured him that it was indeed visibility zero and completely unskiable. "As a matter of fact, the mountain is closed due to high winds," one of his buddies reported. With the help of Delta ground personnel, he was able to secure a new flight at four in the afternoon the following day. Trying to turn lemons into lemonade, he taxied into the Vegas strip, luckily scored a room at the Luxor Hotel, and got a massage to ease his tension. By 10:00 p.m., he had enjoyed a dinner at Alizé and was up four thousand dollars at the roulette table.

At noon, he called Delta to ascertain whether his flight was delayed, at which time he learned that the Wyoming blizzard had spread to a three-hundred-mile radius and had also shuttered most airports in Colorado and Utah. Yes, his flight would be delayed twenty-four hours.

The afternoon margaritas by the Luxor pool were quite refreshing. By early evening, he had made reservations to the Cirque du Soleil show, and then he hit the gaming tables again. Here, he gained another $5,200, thanks in part to Crystal, a rather top-heavy blonde, who regularly kissed his dice and claimed to be his lucky charm. She proved to be just that during the night even though it cost Bernstein four hundred newly acquired dollars.

By the time she had left at 10:00 a.m., Ronald enjoyed his room service eggs Benedict with truffle fries, and then he called his friends in Jackson Hole. "What's up?"

"Still a whiteout," his buddy reported. "But it's supposed to clear by noon. Maybe you can still get a flight—"

"Too late," Ronald interrupted. "At this point, I say, 'Let it snow. Let it snow, Let it snow.'" He then redialed Crystal, set up another lucky charm for the upcoming evening, and promised himself he would relive the experience the next year. Thanks to Google, he actually did book his flight to Jackson Hole on the most weather-cancelled weekend of the year. Just in case, he booked a backup plane to Vegas.

Bobbing
Watercolor
27 × 22
2009

Bobbing

I don't actually like fishing, and never did. C'mon, it's not a sport. You sit on a pier and wait for something to happen, rather like an endless morning at
the DMV.

Even as a young boy, I assumed it amounted to nothing more than gazing at a lake for several hours until one of those little red-and-white floating bobbers would submerge below water level, supposedly signaling the chance to hook a seven-inch flounder (which must be thrown back because it is not enough "inches.")

"Bobby, keep your eyes on those bobbers," my dad would remind me, as if they might plunge and jump at any second.

"This is boring," I remember protesting after a half hour of nothing.

"What's boring about having a morning out with your dad?" Robert "Bob" M. Rockwell corrected me with an undeniable tinge of parental criticism.

After a few more minutes of actionless fishing, my dad understood the essence of timing. He looked at the sky, then smiled at me. After an uncomfortable gap of silence, he asked me, "Got a girlfriend?"

"Dad, I'm only thirteen!" I protested, as if that would be a sufficient retort.

After a pause, my dad repeated the question. At that time, I was hoping for a ripple in the water to suggest that I might actually have a bite on my fishing line. Unfortunately, the water was placid; and after at least thirty seconds, I felt the need to respond in some way.

After a hem and a haw, I spoke about Becky, my super-cute classmate that had miraculously begun to sprout tits and had actually winked at me in class.

This led to one of the best and most telling conversations I ever had with my dad. I realized that he actually had girlfriends before Mom. I came to understand that he honestly wanted me to enjoy the company of young girls but also be respectful of them. And he talked with me about condoms! Yikes! Embarassing! More than embarassing, way, way, way too personal.

"I'm hoping I will soon catch something," I remember interrupting him, as I looked back at the still water, in the hopes of changing the subject.

"Keep your eye on that bobber," my dad said, somehow confident that he had effectively made his points about life, love, and laughing in the face of the wind.

Quite honestly, I don't remember whether I ever caught a flounder on that day. I do remember never getting to first base with Becky. And I definitely remember my dad snapping his fingers and singing along to Bobby Darin's "Somewhere Beyond the Sea" as we drove home from the pier in his open-topped '85 Miata.

Acccording to psychologists, kids end up inevitably repeating the behavior of their parents. On the minor points, I disagree:

My dad was a marketing guy. I am an academic.

My dad was a Yankee fan. I follow the Mets.

My dad was a skier. I like the beach.

My dad found a way to talk to his son. Until today, I had not figured that out.

"Robbie," I told my boy. "Keep an eye on that bobber. If it dips below sea level, you will have a catch."

"This is boring," my twelve-year-old son sighed while he constantly dialed new Facebook, e-mail, LinkedIn, Twitter Nextdoor, and other social networks.

"Got a girlfriend?" I asked and watched him momentarily cease his nonstop texting.

Over the next two hours, we spoke about female respect, safe sex, gay–lesbian relationships, even father–son relatonships. In the process, I figured out why men supposedly "fish." And while my son, Robbie, had never heard of the classic, I again enjoyed a CD of Bobby Darin singing "Somewhere Beyond the Sea."

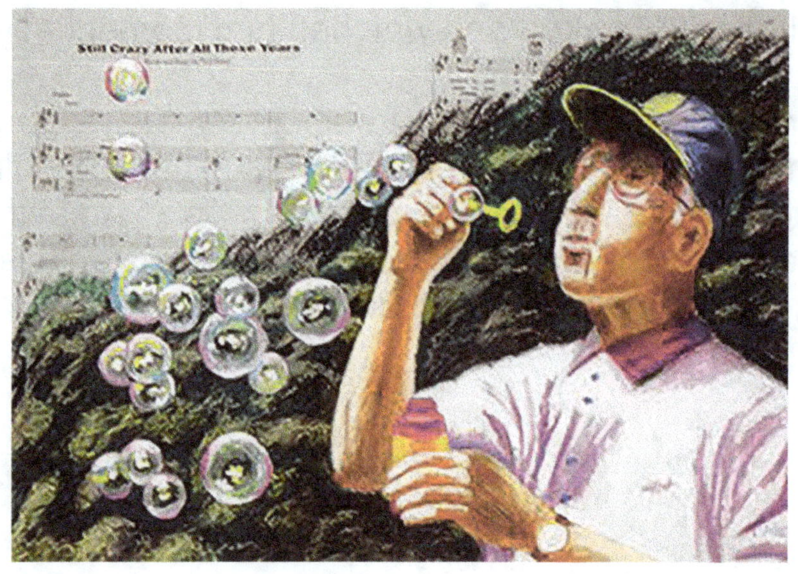

Still Crazy
Pastel
30 × 24
2003

The Bubble Break

Maury Rosen dipped his yellow plastic wand in the bottle of soapy liquid and tilted his head back. He then filled his lungs and streamed a slow, steady breath into the circle of iridescence. As had happened for the past ten minutes, it filled the atmosphere with seven or eight bubbles. Again and again, Maury had to giggle as the fragile orbs floated in the air and occasionally collided with each other.

The seventy-one-year-old was not daft. If anything, he was saner than all his other coworkers who were lighting up Pall Malls, Camel Filters, and Salem Menthols outside the R. J. Reynolds headquarters in Winston-Salem, North Carolina.

As RJR's chief legal counsel for the past forty years, Rosen was several years past the suggested retirement age. However, he was now widely regarded as a visionary legend within the conglomerate. Ironically, three decades ago, the man was considered a turncoat when he recommended that the tobacco giant increase its disclosure of possible health risks, limit its appeal to teenagers, and diversify— hopefully into Oreos, vanilla wafers, and other user-friendly snacks.

"Wanna drag?" Doug Cavanaugh, his coworker for the past fifteen years, said and offered an extended Winston Light from the gold-colored package.

"Are you kidding?" Maury laughed as he again dipped the plastic wand into the bubble water.

"Yes," Doug responded and lit up his favorite brand. After a long, satisfying drag, the junior partner asked, "How long has it been?"

Maury expelled at least eight new airborne wobbly spheres and watched each precarious trajectory. "Thirty years," the chief counsel answered.

"Why?" the employee asked. It was a question that vexed him for several decades.

"Why what?"

"Why take advantage of a smoke break if you don't smoke?"

Maury blew another eight bubbles. "I value this moment in our mornings and afternoons. In fact, I think they are perhaps the most important ten minutes in any workday. You and I learn about our wives and daughters and grandkids. We admit our own noncorporate feelings and sometimes our deepest vulnerabilities. Sometimes, it gives us a chance to talk about what pisses us off about each other. Every once in a while, we even get the chance to tell a joke or two."

"Yeah, that's the beauty of a smoke break," Doug agreed and then took the last drag of his Winston.

Maury took another deep breath and blew out eight more multicolored bubbles. "That's why I choose to have an alternative oral/physical/tactile experience outside the corporate door . . . so I can take advantage of the bonding experience without hazard."

Despite the fact that Doug Cavanaugh liked and admired his boss, he seemed to resent the nonsmoking advice, at least on this particular day. With some aggression, he snuffed out the butt in the outdoor ashtray and suggested, "Maybe the smoke break is worth preserving."

"I would call it a bubble break," Maury offered.

"It's a little crazy," Doug rebutted.

"It's an excuse for something more important," Maury countered.

His longtime friend stormed through the revolving doors of RJR and then looked back across the glass at his friend and mentor. He then rejoined
the argument.

"I have more to say," the junior partner protested.

"Have at it," Maury Rosen said and happily extended his yellow pipe to his favorite protégé. "Blow off some steam," the chief legal counsel advised. What ensued was their first nonsmoking smoke break. Not as nicotine-rich as a shared cigarette, but every bit as satisfying as a "what's up with you, what's up with me" dialogue.

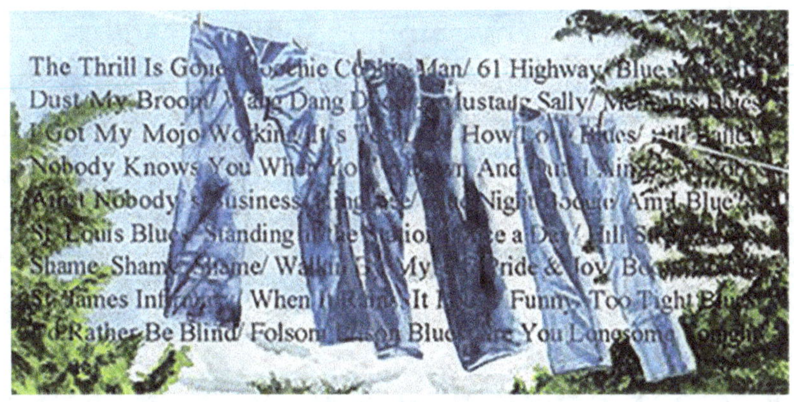

Favorite Blues
Watercolor
32 × 20
2007

Favorite Blues

Xavier Marquis couldn't dribble a basketball or compute Euclidean geometry, but he could play a mean saxophone. It didn't impress most of his rap-happy friends in Mt. Vernon, New York. However, it was an amazing oasis for the young teenager and a swelling source of pride for his mother, Zia, who had generously paid for lessons since the boy was six years old.

Every Thursday evening, Zia would drive her son to Sam Ash's music store in nearby White Plains and would patiently wait in the store during his one-hour lesson. Invariably, young Xavier would eventually bound out of his practice room and beam with newfound confidence. During the week, he would practice without prompting.

Last year, Zia did have a private progress-report conversation with her son's instructor. The man gushed. "The kid has a gift," the middle-aged sax teacher said. "He has a natural knack for the blues, and if you are agreeable, I might be able to get him a gig in Harlem."

"Harlem?" Zia sighed. Having fled this neighborhood for a better life in Westchester County, it was not the answer she wanted.

"It's a good band. And he's a good kid. They will take care of him. And by the way, it is not the Harlem you and I left behind twenty years ago."

After hemming and hawing for two weeks (and with some "please, please, please" encouragement from Xavier), Zia agreed to drive him down to 135th Street for a two-hour audition/practice. After seventy minutes, the bandleader, Tyrone Williams, walked into the street and looked for a woman sitting behind the wheel of a 2007 Toyota.

"Zia," the man asked after tapping on the driver-side window. "We could use a good saxophonist like Xavier. It's all classic blues. We are not a rock band. But this kid knows how to speak through his instrument. My advice? He should be allowed to have his voice heard."

The mother agreed to think about it and was intent on a long heart-to-heart with her only son.

"The band is a bunch of old guys," Zia began with some pique in her voice. "But I did like the band leader who came out to speak to me."

"They are the best blues band in the city," Xavier answered.

"And you like their music?"

"I prefer to think of it as my music."

After at least an uncomfortable fifteen-second pause, the mother considered her son's passion and the sacrifice that it would entail. The boy simply looked at his mother for approval. She not only fully understood her son's talent and ambition but also accepted her role as the one single parent who must look beyond the immediate horizon.

"Xavier, I do not have much money," she struggled. "But what I have is yours, and I will do anything for you to achieve greatness. If you want to attend CCNY or Stony Brook or New Paltz, I will make it happen, because I believe in you." After a breath, she added, "You could be the first college graduate in this family."

The young man sighed and then countered without the slightest bit of hesitation. "I could also be the first member of this family to ever play in New Orleans or Chicago or New York City or wherever the Blue Master Band will play.

They want me. And I am good enough."

After a two-hour tear fest, Mom agreed, on one condition. "Promise me, you will never take advantage of a young woman. Promise me you will read books. Promise me you will not wear those oversized blue jeans below your butt as if it's a cool thing to attract sluts."

Xavier laughed aloud. "At least, I can promise you count number 3. Matter of fact, I guarantee that will be the case. After all, I will be playing with middle-aged masters," Xavier responded. "Mom, they are not ghetto blasters!"

The next morning, Zia washed and dried all three Levi's she had bought for her son. She then packed them in his luggage, along with T-shirts, underwear, socks and a private letter.

When Xavier opened it on his bus ride down to New Orleans, he was so proud to be raised by Zia Marquis. It read, "Someday, maybe you will be famous. If not, you will be happy, especially when I come to witness your magic in the next three months. Let me know when the time is right."

After working fifteen hours a day, Xavier invited his mom to come down to the delta last weekend. As she would readily admit, it was more amazing than any commencement speech from any university.

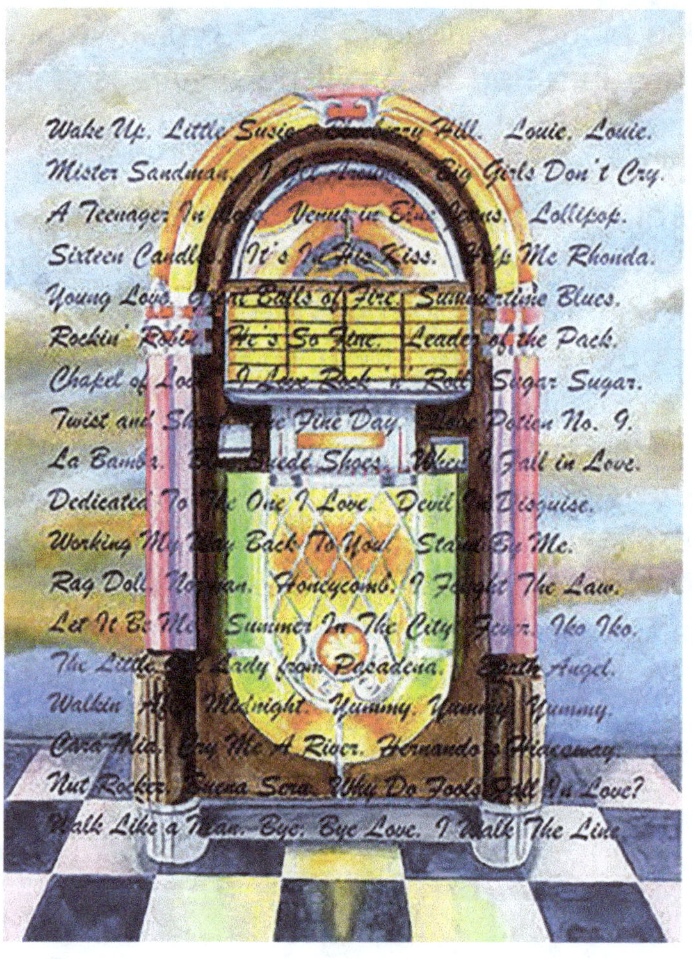

Jukebox Heaven
Watercolor
28 × 31
2010

Jukebox Heaven

Unlike the typical "knock, knock," there was a rhythmic, syncopated tap on the door, with a few bangs at the top, countered by a bass beat on the bottom.

Within five seconds, a bearded man in a white robe opened that thick wooden portal and then the pearlescent iron gate. He extended his hand to the newcomer and introduced himself. "I am Peter," the greeter succinctly said, as if his first name should be sufficient. "And you are . . ." the questioner put on his reading glasses, took his clipboard, and scanned down the computer printout.

"I'm Johnny," the visitor somberly answered, thinking that first names were undoubtedly the custom in this new venue.

Peter looked at the man dressed in black. "Uh-huh," he responded skeptically and continued to turn the pages of his check-in files. "What has been your business? Your impact? In other words, what qualifies you?"

"I don't know," Johnny humbly answered. "I just made music the best I could."

Peter flipped a few more pages on his clipboard and then seemed to recognize the visitor. This reservationist could not resist a slight wry smile. He then looked back at the modest man, just to make sure the dossier and the image matched. "Well, you have definitely had a few stumbles along the way."

"More than a few," Johnny answered.

"But you did make amazing music," Peter quickly responded and then looked at his checklist. "We appreciate that here. What was the purpose? Fame?"

Johnny chortled. "Nah, it's always a long, hard slog to fame."

"Money?"

"There was no money until I was in my fifties."

"Girls?"

"There was only one girl that mattered. Her name was June."

By now, Peter was busily marking the computer sheet with his own grading scheme. As Johnny stood before him, the receptionist mumbled, "Some troubles. Made amends. Jukebox hits. Yes, jukebox. One. Two. Three. Four. Free concerts. That counts. That's big." Peter then high-fived the visitor and waved him forward.

"What's jukebox have to do with it?" Johnny innocently asked.

"It means you brought pleasure and above-the-earth melodies to millions."

"And that counts?"

"Big-time. It's godlike, and those concerts at Folsom were major. As the Big Guy says, 'Whatever you do for the least of my brethren, you do for me.'" Peter then gave a thumbs-up gesture and encouraged him to speed through the portal.

Never one to bask in the spotlight, Johnny squinted in the glare as he walked through the gates with the man called Peter and felt a new creative inspiration.

"Is June here?" he asked.

"Yes, of course. She put up with you."

"What about Ritchie Valens?"

"Definitely."

"Elvis?"

"He was an amazing talent and good to his staff. So on balance, yes."

"What about John Lennon?"

"Well, the Big Guy didn't particularly like the fact that he said the group was bigger than Jesus, but he did understand the ironic critique and loved 'Hey Jude.'"

After a pause, Johnny viewed the sunrise and the Great Jukebox in the sky. He then asked the receptionist, "So I'm in?"

"Two conditions," Peter said. "You've got to lose that man-in-black thing."

John put on the white robe that the angels on his right and left extended to him. "And you've got to promise to be good in your own way. No transgressions. No failures. No excuses," Peter demanded.

Johnny took the guitar the angel extended to him and began singing the iconic song "I Walk the Line." In the vast, miles-long audience, many reformed members of Folsom Prison cheered and were again so happy to be in his company.

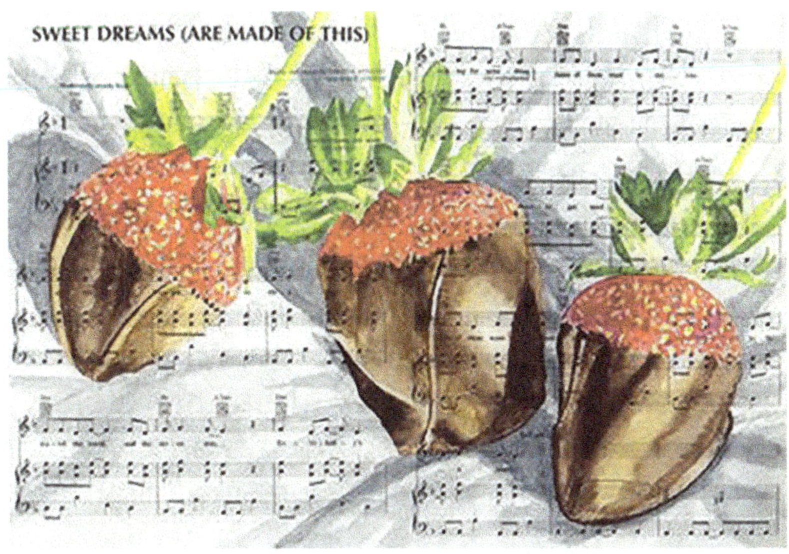

Sweet Dreams
Watercolor
23 × 18
2013

Sweet Dreams

When my receptionist informed me that Scarlett Johansson would be my next patient, I admit to succumbing to a rare bout of vanity. I ducked into my private bathroom to inspect my hair so it didn't look too plastered. I splashed some water on my cheeks to refresh my face and then returned to my desk to shuffle some papers as if I was diagnosing my last visitor.

When I looked up, I said, "Thanks, Mindy," to my middle-aged receptionist who had escorted the stunning young starlet into my office. I then shook Scarlett's soft hand and invited her to sit in the nearest wing chair. "How did you hear of me, Ms. Johansson?" I asked.

"Call me Scarlett, please," she responded.

"How did you hear about me, Scarlett?"

"I think it was that recent feature story in the *Malibu Times*," she said and flashed that now-famous shy smile. "Or maybe it was a recent conversation I had with Ryan Gosling. Or perhaps Javier Bardem."

"I have treated them both," I admitted and laughed about that puff piece in my local newspaper. It was titled "Dream Catcher of the

Stars," and it described, in glowing terms, my practice as a licensed dream therapist, using subconscious psychological fantasies to unlock the mysteries of one's life. "Why don't you tell me what you're experiencing," I encouraged her.

"It's a little embarrassing," the young woman admitted.

I assured her that everything said in my office would be strictly confidential and gestured for her to proceed. I could see her look over to the door to make sure that it was firmly closed so as to ensure that no other patients could overhear her story. "I've had this dream several times," she leaned toward me and whispered. "I am in a bedroom with Eva Mendes, and we are both in very sheer negligees."

"Have you met? Do you know Eva Mendes?" I asked dispassionately.

"Only in these dreams. And as far as I know, neither of us is a lesbian. Anyway, we walk to this bed, and there on the pillow are three plump Godiva chocolate–covered strawberries."

"Three," I repeat and take notes.

"One for me. One for Eva. And one for a very special male guest."

"I see. And do you know this man? This third person?"

"I do now," she answered. She paused and then looked me in the eye,
"It's you."

I remember laughing out loud. I reminded her that until five minutes ago, she had absolutely no idea what I looked like. She rebutted that the *Malibu Times* photo was a very good likeness.

Wow, in my twenty-year career, I had heard hundreds of dreams, but I must say this was the first one in which I myself was a featured player. "It might have been someone who bore a slight resemblance to me." I shrugged.

"No, it was you. Definitely you," Scarlett responded. Then she teased, "Would you like to know what happened next?"

Reluctantly, and rather unprofessionally, I nodded and urged her to continue. She then described a remarkable three-way sexual encounter worthy of a triple-X rating.

It was the first and only time I encountered Scarlett, or Eva Mendes for that matter. In the midst of screaming "More, more," my wife of twenty-two years (who looked remarkably like Mindy the receptionist) woke me from this once-in-a-lifetime reverie.

"What were you dreaming, Herb?" she asked.

"I can't quite remember," I lied while vividly recalling every frame. I then showered, shaved, and put on my uniform for my day ahead as assistant manager at the Foot Locker store.

Before going home that night, I bought some chocolate-covered strawberries in the hopes that it might somehow trigger a return engagement with Scarlett and Eva.

No such luck.

Instead, the gift was interpreted as a romantic gesture by my wife, who was surprisingly adventurous in bed that evening.

It wasn't bad. But I must admit, it wasn't the same.

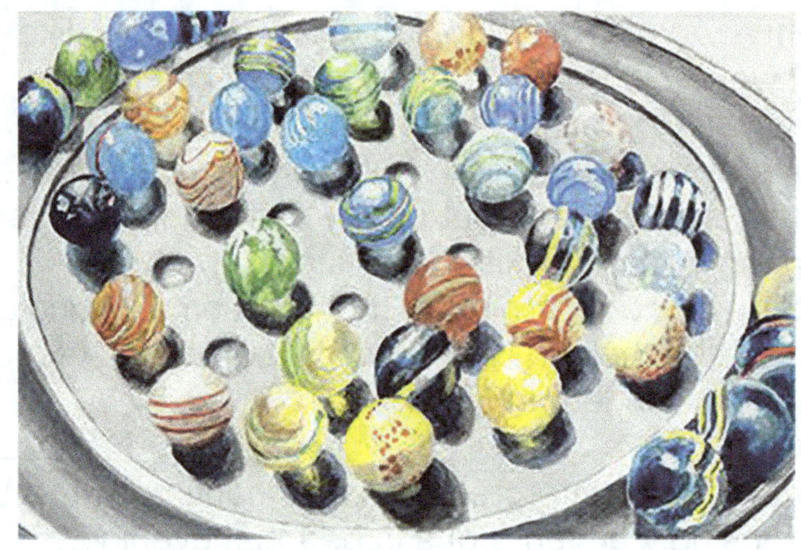

Solitaire

Ever since she buried her husband, eighty-seven-year-old Millie Hendricks had become something of a recluse. It's not that she was completely alone in her St. Petersburg condo. She had the constant companionship of Esmeralda, her big orange tabby cat. The widow had her daily trips to Winn-Dixie supermarket to get her weekly groceries and cat supplies. And she had her solitaire games in the marble set given to her by her late husband, Albert.

A year after his heart attack, Millie did try more frequent forays into town on the senior bus. There were shopping tours with other senior women at the malls, but Millie was never a clotheshorse, and besides, most of the fashions were decades too outrageous for her. For a while, she tried the weekly bingo games but tired of the winning orgasmic screams from women of her own age (even so, she still attended the event every month or so just to feel somewhat connected with her contemporaries).

As she brought out the board at 10:00 a.m. this morning on her small dining room table, Millie removed the center marble and began her mental and strategic challenge of the day. After several "jumps," she studied the ebony board and took a sighing pause.

"What do you think, Esmeralda? I have several choices. To the right, I have a shortcut that will leave the left half of the board in a traffic jam of marbles. To the left, I have a clearer path but a potentially less exciting path." The cat, sitting on the mahogany table as she often did during these one-on-self combats, just looked at her companion and then seemed mesmerized by the stream of sunlight coming into the small apartment.

Within the next three seconds, the telephone rang.

After taking one more look at the vexing choice of marble movement, Millie walked to the nearby wall phone and picked up the receiver after four rings.

It was her only daughter, Dora, who made her weekly obligatory call to Mom from her comfy home in Atlanta. In some ways, it was a typical update. Yes, Dora was still golfing once a month. She was still busy with her gardening. And as usual, there was the usual planted notion that it might be time for Mom to think about "a different living situation for your own safety and companionship needs." But then there was a rather atypical curveball. "I'd like to come down and see you for a few weeks?" Dora asked.

"What's a few weeks mean? Two?" Millie asked.

"Yeah, I was thinking it might be nice."

"When?"

"May."

"Let me look on my calendar," Millie replied and then walked over to the unfinished game board. After a few minutes, she returned to the phone. "Those dates look clear," she replied.

After settling on dates, the older woman hung up the phone and peered into her small apartment. Esmeralda, sitting on the window ledge and enjoying the streams of sunlight, seemed to sense that it was time to return to the game table.

The old woman knew what this upcoming trip would mean. Consequently, she x-ed out her bimonthly bingo game on May 12. On that same calendar, she made a May 1 note to stock up for Dora at Winn-Dixie. She also anticipated that there would be further discussion about moving into "a home." However, that reasoned reply could wait.

At the present time, Millie Hendricks was facing a defining choice in front of her witness/companion / silent partner. The old woman looked at her cat. "Esmeralda, what do you think? Left or right?" When the tabby slowly moved her head toward the sunlight, Millie just sighed. "Albert would know and would say which route to take," she admonished her cat.

After moving the aqua marble over the dark-blue speckled one, the old woman completed her moves and the game. Then she sat alone at the dining room table. She promised herself she would not talk aloud to Albert or Esmeralda in front of her daughter. Otherwise, a daily debate about "a home" would occupy every day. And as Millie had often told her daughter, "I'll think about that option when I turn ninety-five."

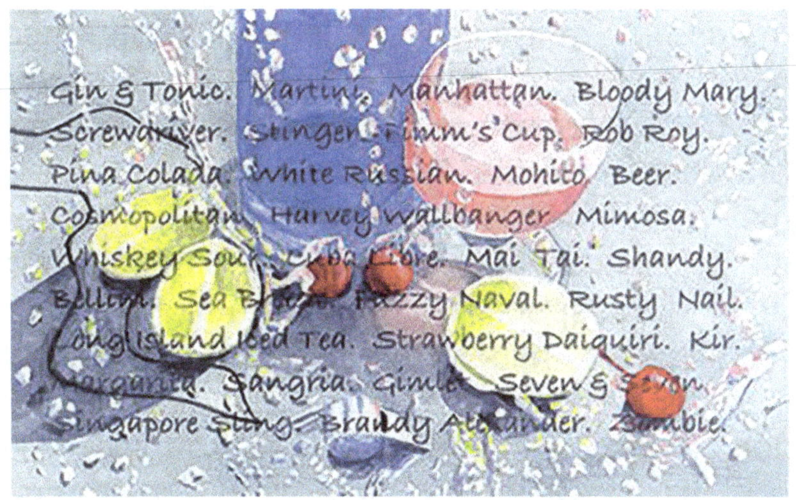

Wet Your Whistle
Watercolor
35 × 24
2011

Wet Your Whistle

Ever since Otto Dingledine had seen the movie *Cocktail*, he wanted that exhilarating, fast-paced, sexually explosive lifestyle. Forget the fact that the majority of the movie was set in sybaritic Jamaica. Forget the fact the Tom Cruise, in his prime, was flexing his muscles with every poured bottle of rum. Forget the fact that it's a goddamn movie.

"Looks fun," he told the admissions director of the Cleveland Bartending Academy.

"It's hard work too," the obese attendant replied.

"I'll be the judge of that," Otto chortled, as if his smartass response was worthy of Jimmy Fallon's late-night talk show.

It had taken the young man a few years to get to this point. After high school, he enrolled in the junior college to up his mediocre grades. After a single semester of subpar performance, he got a job in the warehouse of a lumberyard—stacking studs, plywood, and quarter rounds. As Otto often told his local bartender, it did not afford him the opportunity to shine and utilize his outgoing personality.

"Right," the bartender smiled and wiped the bar.

"I'll have another beer. No, wait a minute, make that a brewski." Otto laughed aloud, showcasing his dim trademark wit.

At 8:00 a.m. the next morning, he was the first attendee at the two-week bartending college. He had arrived a full half hour before starting time but was intent on making a good impression, which was why he wore a bow tie on that first day of class. There were twelve other students in attendance, equally divided between hot-looking young women, a few normal guys, and three or four dorks like Otto Dingledine; so in that respect, he did not feel alone.

The teacher, a jaded, middle-aged man who looked a little like Kevin Kline, explained the basics on day 1—ice, refrigeration, sanitation (don't use your fingers to grab the ice), simple syrup, hooking up a beer keg, decanting wine, single malt versus blended, etc. The next day, they learned two-ingredient basics like vodka tonics, rum and Cokes, and scotch and water. From that, it progressed to negronis, mojitos, Singapore Slings, Rusty Nails, and other exotic concoctions.

Every night, Otto studied the recipes and proportions and occasionally made a few exhibits for his mom, who generally passed out after two samples.

After ten days, it was time for the big test. In the space of ten minutes, each student would be required to make eight different drinks, each randomly pulled out of a hat. Through some ridiculous alignment of the stars, Otto drew the easiest drinks known to mankind and miraculously passed the final exam.

"Yowsa, yowsa!" he screamed upon viewing his passing score. He then looked at his fellow students. "I'm tellin' ya, I'm gonna give Tom Cruise a run for his money. Look out, Katie Holmes," he yelped with a rather embarrassing karate kick, as if that relationship ever had the slightest chance.

As promised, Otto had placement interviews. On most, the bow tie did not bode well, but at Applebee's, they seemed to appreciate his Orville Redenbacher persona. It gave him the chance to work behind the bar for two weeks until his grating personality garnered too many negatives from the "How did we do" comment cards.

From this résumé-building experience, he was able to secure a job at a place called Blarney Rock, which was basically a hangout for senior citizen barflies. "Hey, let me wet your whistle, assuming you still can whistle," he joked to an unemployed seventy-five-year-old the other day with that fake finger / gunshot pantomime that you never see other than in bad mafia movies. Two days later, Otto was bounced from this place too.

Fortunately, in this economy, he is back at the lumberyard. These days, he doesn't often shuck and jive with the few customers he is allowed to meet. However, he is more than happy to challenge his fellow coworkers with how to make the perfect mojito. Unfortunately, with a variety of excuses, none of them have ever accepted his invitation to visit him and his mom. Still, the bartender college graduate rehearses the recipes night after night. Sometimes, he even attempts to twirl the bottles.

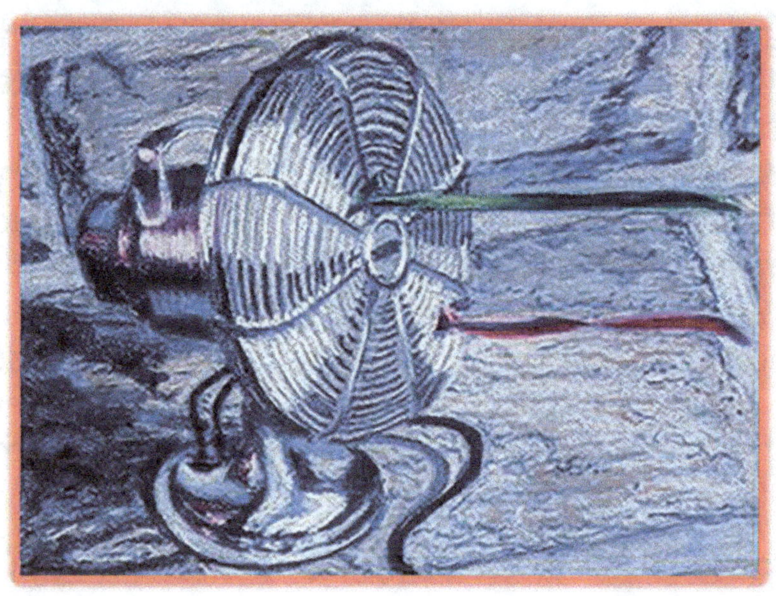

The Coolest Time of the Year

Many of my friends love spring. When the first daffodils, irises, and hyacinths appear in early April, they are quick to call it their favorite season. Of course, all that optimism normally fades by April 10, when they must file their annual income tax.

Others adore late August—flip-flops, suntan, a house full of the kids' friends night after night, breakfast and laundry for the kids' friends day after day, college tuitions due. Ah, if only we could limit it to flip-flops.

Still others prefer Thanksgiving—the time when family members who do not get along get together to argue about politics and gorge on turkey, stuffing, and pumpkin pie.

And then there is Christmas.

As a young kid, it was always my favorite, coolest time of the year. Yeah, part of it was the fact that I was raised in Vermont, where the snow-covered fields and hot cocoa make you feel like you are living inside the best Christmas movie ever made. But the appeal of the season always went beyond temperature.

As I think back on it, what's not to love as an eight-year-old? You've got Santa, cookies, gifts, carols, parties, neighbors, cousins, cards, hugs, and (maybe the best thing of all) a long Christmas vacation from school.

Of course, a lot of that has gone by the boards in my past fifty years on this planet. Rest assured, I am not quite at the curmudgeon stage, but I do find myself tiring of the seasons, especially since so much has changed for me in the past several decades.

Perhaps this is the time to explain my personal situation. Brace yourself for a "bah, humbug" downer (unless you have a fascination with dark humor). The first chink in the Christmas armor came when my husband of twenty-three years announced that he had fallen in love with his fellow carpenter, a veritable stud named Gordon. Partly to compensate, I found solace with a female restaurateur in town named Rachel, but in retrospect, it was pure retaliation. Deep down, I prefer guys. My only child, a daughter named Iris (hooray for spring!) wanted to be a single mom and move to Portland, Oregon.

At this point, I thought it was time to say good-bye to chilly Vermont and hello to hot, hot, hot Dania, Florida. In my fantasies, I thought it could be a fresh start. However, everyone here is eighty and plays shuffleboard.

Christmas will be different, I tell myself. Yes, it is. These days, no one makes cookies with nuts because everyone is allergic. If possible, the cookies should be vegan.

These days, there are no Christmas carols. Anything that conjures the faintest religious overtone is overruled in the interest of political correctness. Consequently, we sing "When You Wish upon a Star." Hey, let's make Walt Disney the modern-day Santa Claus!

Fewer and fewer people send Christmas cards. And when they are sent, they are accompanied by a bland message, "Best wishes at this time of year."

And gifts? For the past seven years, my daughter has sent me an Amazon.com alternative book selection. Wow! Just to add icing on the cake, it's now eighty-three degrees in Dania. Instead of a Christmas tree, I have a small fan with green and red ribbons attached to the frame, blowing air in the general direction of my non-air-conditioned room.

"Hello?" I answered the out-of-the-blue phone call.

"It's Iris," she says. "Can I bring Chloe to visit you this Christmas?"

"Two days from now?"

"Chloe needs to know what an old-fashioned Christmas is like, and no one knows how to do that better than you, Mom."

In the next twenty-four hours, I buy dozens of presents. I stock up on CDs of Dean Martin, Michael Bublé, and Celine Dion singing old-time carols. I cut red and green paper and make a homemade card for my daughter and my granddaughter. I make some Christmas biscotti with pistachios (hey, don't eat them if you are allergic). And I hug.

Suddenly, after all these years, like my eight-year-old grandchild, I must admit: it's just the coolest time of the year.